MY VIEW OF THE WORLD

By the same Author

WHAT IS LIFE?
SCIENCE AND HUMANISM
SPACE-TIME STRUCTURE
STATISTICAL THERMODYNAMICS
NATURE AND THE GREEKS
MIND AND MATTER
EXPANDING UNIVERSES

ERWIN SCHRÖDINGER

MY VIEW OF THE WORLD

Translated from the German by
CECILY HASTINGS

CAMBRIDGE
AT THE UNIVERSITY PRESS
1964

PUBLISHED BY
THE SYNDICS OF THE CAMBRIDGE UNIVERSITY PRESS

Bentley House, 200 Euston Road, London, N.W. 1
American Branch: 32 East 57th Street, New York 22, N.Y.
West African Office: P.O. Box 33, Ibadan, Nigeria

©

PAUL ZSOLNAY VERLAG GMBH
HAMBURG-VIENNA, 1961

ENGLISH TRANSLATION
©
CAMBRIDGE UNIVERSITY PRESS, 1964

Printed in Great Britain at the University Printing House, Cambridge
(Brooke Crutchley, University Printer)

CONTENTS

FOREWORD *page* vii

SEEK FOR THE ROAD

I	Metaphysics in general	3
II	A cheerless balance-sheet	7
III	Philosophical wonder	10
IV	The problem	12
V	The Vedantic vision	18
VI	An exoteric introduction to scientific thought	23
VII	More about non-plurality	30
VIII	Consciousness, organic, inorganic, mneme	38
IX	On becoming conscious	45
X	The moral law	52

WHAT IS REAL?

I	Reasons for abandoning the dualism of thought and existence, or mind and matter	61

Contents

II	Linguistic information and our common possession of the world	page 67
III	The imperfection of understanding	82
IV	The doctrine of identity: light and shadow	92
V	Two grounds for astonishment: pseudo-ethics	104

FOREWORD

The two essays here published for the first time are separated by an interval of thirty-five years. The first and longer one was written shortly before my appointment as Max Planck's successor in Berlin, and a few months before the idea of what is now called wave mechanics began for a while to monopolise my whole interest; the second and shorter one dates from two years after my appointment as Professor Emeritus at the University of Vienna. The two are closely related in theme, and, of course, also connect with many ideas which I have publicly advocated in the intervening period.

I do not know whether it is presumptuous of me to suppose that readers will be interested in 'my' view of the world. The critics, not myself, will decide on this. But a gesture of decorous modesty is usually in fact a disguise for arrogance. I should prefer not to be guilty of this. Anyway, the total (I have counted) is about twenty-eight to twenty-nine thousand words. Not an excessive size for a view of the world.

There is one complaint which I shall not escape. Not a word is said here of acausality, wave mechanics, indeterminacy relations, complementarity, an expanding universe, continuous creation, etc. Why doesn't he talk about what he knows instead of trespassing on the professional philosopher's preserves? *Ne sutor supra crepidam.* On this I can cheerfully justify myself: because I do not think that these things have as much connection as is

Foreword

currently supposed with a philosophical view of the world. I think that I see eye to eye here, on certain essential points, with Max Planck and Ernst Cassirer. In 1918, when I was thirty-one, I had good reason to expect a chair of theoretical physics at Czernowitz (in succession to Geitler). I was prepared to do a good job lecturing on theoretical physics, with, as my supreme model, the magnificent lectures given by my beloved teacher Fritz Hasenöhrl, who had been killed in the War; but for the rest, to devote myself to philosophy, being deeply imbued at the time with the writings of Spinoza, Schopenhauer, Mach, Richard Semon and Richard Avenarius. My guardian angel intervened: Czernowitz soon no longer belonged to Austria. So nothing came of it. I had to stick to theoretical physics, and, to my astonishment, something occasionally emerged from it. So this little book is really the fulfilment of a very long cherished wish.

E.S.

ALPBACH
July 1960

PUBLISHER'S NOTE

The Syndics of the Cambridge University Press are greatly indebted to Professor O. R. Frisch for his help in the preparation of this edition.

SEEK FOR THE ROAD

Wo Rätsel mich zu neuen Rätseln führten
Da wussten *sie* die Wahrheit ganz genau.
GRILLPARZER

Where riddles led me on to further riddles,
To *them* the truth was quite precisely known.

AUTUMN, 1925

I
METAPHYSICS IN GENERAL

It is relatively easy to sweep away the whole of metaphysics, as Kant did. The slightest puff in its direction blows it away, and what was needed was not so much a powerful pair of lungs to provide the blast, as a powerful dose of courage to turn it against so timelessly venerable a house of cards.

But you must not think that what has then been achieved is the actual elimination of metaphysics from the empirical content of human knowledge. In fact, if we cut out all metaphysics it will be found to be vastly more difficult, indeed probably quite impossible, to give any intelligible account of even the most circumscribed area of specialisation within any specialised science you please. Metaphysics includes, amongst other things—to take just one quite crude example— the unquestioning acceptance of a more-than-physical —that is, transcendental—significance in a large number of thin sheets of wood-pulp covered with black marks such as are now before you.

Or, to take it at a deeper level: call to mind that sense of misgiving, that cold clutch of dreary emptiness which comes over everybody, I expect, when they first encounter the description given by Kirchhoff and Mach of the task of physics (or of science generally): 'a description of the facts, with the maximum of completeness and the maximum economy of thought'; a feeling of emptiness which one cannot master, despite the emphatic and even enthusiastic agreement with which one's theoretical reason can hardly fail to accept this prescription. In actual fact (let us examine ourselves honestly and faithfully), to have *only* this goal before one's eyes would not suffice to keep the work of research going forward in any field whatsoever. A real elimination of metaphysics means taking the soul out of *both* art *and* science, turning them into skeletons incapable of any further development.

But theoretical metaphysics *has* been eliminated. There is no appeal against Kant's sentence. Philosophy of the post-Kantian period—perhaps right down to our own day—has shown us the tormented writhings of the long-drawn-out death agony of metaphysics.

Speaking as a scientist, it seems to me that it is our uncommonly difficult task, as post-Kantians, on the one hand step by step to erect barriers which will restrain the influence of metaphysics on the presentation of facts seen as true within our individual fields—while on the other hand preserving it as the indispensable basis of our knowledge, both general and particular. It is the apparent contradiction in this which is our problem. We might say, to use an image, that as we go forward on the road of knowledge we have *got* to let ourselves be guided by the invisible hand of metaphysics reaching out to us from the mist, but that we must always be on our guard lest its soft seductive pull should draw us from the road into an abyss. Or, to look at it another way: among the advancing hosts of the forces of knowledge, metaphysics is the vanguard, establishing the forward outposts in an unknown hostile territory; we cannot do without such outposts, but we all know that they are exposed to the most extreme danger. Or again: metaphysics does not form part of the house of knowledge but is the scaffolding, without which further construction is impossible. Perhaps we may even be permitted to say: metaphysics turns into physics in the course of its development—but not of course in the sense in which it might have seemed to do so before Kant. *Never*, that is, by a gradual establishing of initially uncertain opinions, but always through a clarification of, and change in, the philosophical point of view.

How we are to come to terms with the announcement that metaphysics is defunct, confronts us as a still more serious and difficult question when we leave the sphere of pure knowledge and consider culture as a whole, including ethical problems. No one, of course, was more aware of this than Kant himself; hence his second critique of reason.

In the course of the last hundred years, the western world has achieved a quite enormous development in one particular direction: that is to say, a thorough knowledge of what underlies natural spatio-temporal events (physics and chemistry) and, based on this, a fantastic abundance of 'mechanisms', in the widest sense, have been constructed to extend the sphere of influence of the human will (technology). I feel impelled to state explicitly at this point that I am very far from holding that *this* (especially the second half of it, technology) is the most significant thing that has been happening in Europe during this period. I think it probable that this age, which delights in calling itself the age of technology, will in some later time be described, in terms of its brightest lights and deepest shadows, as the age of the evolutionary idea, and of the decay of the arts. But this is by the way; I am concerned now with what is the strongest force at work at this moment.

This partial 'elephantiasis' has meant that other lines of development in culture and knowledge, in the western mind or whatever we are to call it, have been neglected, and indeed allowed to decay to a greater degree than ever before. It almost seems as though the one mightily developing organ has exerted a directly damaging and crippling effect on the others. Rising to their feet after centuries of shameful servitude imposed by the Church, conscious of their sacred rights and their divine mission, the natural sciences turned against their ancient tormentress with blows of rage and hatred; heedless that, with all her inadequacies and derelictions of duty, she was still the one and only appointed guardian of our most sacred ancestral heritage. Slowly, almost unobserved, that spark of ancient Indian wisdom, which the marvellous Rabbi had kindled to new flame beside the Jordan, flickered out; the light faded from the re-born sun of Greece, whose rays had ripened the fruits we now enjoy. The people no longer know anything of these things. Most of them have nothing to hold on to and no one to follow. They believe neither in God nor gods; to them the Church is now only a political party, and morality nothing but a burdensome restriction which, without the support of those no longer credible bugbears on which it leant for so long, is now without any basis whatever. A sort of general atavism has set in; western man is in danger of relapsing to an earlier level of development which he has never properly over-

Metaphysics in general

come: crass, unfettered egoism is raising its grinning head, and its fist, drawing irresistible strength from primitive habits, is reaching for the abandoned helm of our ship.

II

A CHEERLESS BALANCE-SHEET

A survey of the final product of western thought, theoretical and practical, over the last fifteen hundred years, is not exactly encouraging. The final conclusion of western wisdom—that all transcendence has got to go, once and for all—is not really applicable in the field of *knowledge* (for which it is actually intended), because we cannot do without metaphysical guidance here: when we think we can, all that is apt to happen is that we replace the grand old metaphysical errors with infinitely more *naïve* and petty ones. On the other hand, in the field of *life* the intellectual middle class has set in motion a practical metaphysical liberation which the noble apostles of that freedom—I mean principally Kant and the philosophers of the Enlightenment—would have shuddered to behold. Our condition, as has often been observed, bears a frightening resemblance to the final stage of the ancient world. And this resemblance does not consist merely in a lack of religion and morals, but precisely in *this* point: that both ages think of themselves as set upon a firm, safe course in the field of pragmatic knowledge, on lines which seem, to the conviction of the age, to be, at least in their general form and basic principles, immune from changes of opinion. Then it was Aristotelian philosophy, now it is modern science. If the likeness holds good here, it is a bad lookout for the present state of affairs! No wonder we lack the courage to accept an inheritance so riddled with liabilities and to pursue a line of thinking that is so obviously going to lead us to bankruptcy, just as it did 2000 years ago.

The deeper you try to go into the character of those universal relations which have always been the subject of philosophy, the less you feel inclined to make any pronouncement about them whatever; because you become ever more aware how unclear, inappropriate, inaccurate and one-sided every pronouncement must be. (This negative attitude has nowhere been so strongly asserted as in Buddhist wisdom, which seeks to give it symbolic expression in such contradictory statements as, for example, a thing is neither A nor not-A, but yet it is not a 'neither A nor not-A', nor can one say that it is 'both A and not-A'.)

What puts one off when examining what are called objective, historical accounts of ancient or modern philosophy, is that one keeps finding such statements as: A or B was a 'representative' of this or that view; so-and-so was an X-ian or a Y-ian, holding allegiance to this system or that, or partly to one and partly to another. Different views are almost always opposed to each other as though they really were *different* views of the *same* object. But this kind of account practically forces us to regard one or other of these thinkers, or both of them, as crazy, or at the very least as totally lacking in judgement. One is then very apt to start

A cheerless balance-sheet

wondering how posterity, including oneself, can possibly think the ill-considered babblings of such blockheads worth any closer attention. But in fact one is dealing, at least in very many cases, with well-founded convictions of highly competent minds, and hence one can be sure that differences in their judgement correspond to differences in the object of it, at least in so far as very different *aspects* of that object were given prominence in their reflective consciousness. A critical account of their thought should, instead of stressing the *contradictions* between them, as is usually done, aim at combining these different aspects into one total picture—needless to say, without compromise, which can only lead to confused and hence *a priori* untrue statements.

The real trouble is this: giving expression to thought by the observable medium of words is like the work of the silkworm. In being made into silk, the material achieves its value. But in the light of day it stiffens; it becomes something alien, no longer malleable. True, we can then more easily and freely recall the same thought, but perhaps we can never experience it again in its original freshness. Hence it is always our latest and deepest insights that are *voce meliora*.

III
PHILOSOPHICAL WONDER

It was said by Epicurus, and he was probably right, that all philosophy takes its origin from θαυμάζειν, philosophical wonder. The man who has never at any time felt consciously struck by the extreme strangeness and oddity of the situation in which we are involved, we know not how, is a man with no affinity for philosophy—and has, by the way, little cause to worry. The unphilosophical and philosophical attitudes can be very sharply distinguished (with scarcely any intermediate forms) by the fact that the first accepts everything that happens as regards its general form, and finds occasion for surprise only in that special content by which something that happens *here today* differs from what happened *there yesterday*; whereas for the second, it is precisely the *common* features of all experience, such as characterise everything we encounter, which are the primary and most profound occasion for astonishment; indeed, one might almost say that it is *the fact that anything is experienced and encountered at all*.

It seems to me that this second type of astonishment—and there is no doubt that it does occur—is itself something very astonishing.

Surely astonishment and wonder are what we feel on encountering something that *differs* from what is *normal*, or at least from what is for some reason or other *expected*. But this whole world is something we encounter only

Philosophical wonder

once. We have nothing with which to compare it, and it is impossible to see how we can approach it with any particular *expectation*. And yet we are astonished; we are puzzled by what we find, yet are unable to say what we should have to have found in order not to be surprised, or how the world would have to have been constructed in order not to constitute a riddle!

Perhaps the lack of any standard of comparison can be felt even more strongly than over θαυμάζειν in general, when we are confronted with the phenomena of philosophical optimism and pessimism. There have been, we know, very notable philosophers—such as Schopenhauer—who have declared that our world is a sad and ill-made place, and there have been others—like Leibniz—who have declared it the best of all conceivable worlds. But what would we say of a man who, having never in all his life left his native village, chose to describe its climate as exceptionally hot or cold?

These phenomena of value judgement, wonder and riddle-finding, which do not refer to any particular aspect of experience but to experience as a whole, and furthermore have impressed themselves not on idiots, but on highly competent minds, seem to me to indicate that we encounter, in our experience, relationships which have never (at least so far), even in their general form, been grasped either by formal logic or, still less, by exact science: relationships which keep forcing us back towards metaphysics; that is, towards something that transcends what is directly accessible to experience—however much we may flourish a death-certificate bearing no less valid a signature than that of Kant himself.

IV

THE PROBLEM

SELF—THE WORLD—DEATH—PLURALITY

If we agree to leave aside, without further discussion, as altogether too naïvely puerile, the idea of a soul dwelling in the body as in a house, quitting it at death, and capable of existing without it, then I think that one of the principal problems, if not *the* principal problem, without whose solution there can be no final peace for the metaphysical urge, can be quite briefly characterised as follows.

Consider these four questions, which cannot, as a whole, be satisfactorily answered with any combination of 'yes' and 'no', but rather lead one on in an endless circle.

(1) Does there exist a Self?
(2) Does there exist a world outside Self?
(3) Does this Self cease with bodily death?
(4) Does the world cease with my bodily death?

If we start with Self, then all the facts of physiology assure us that there is so intimate and necessary a connection between all the sensations of this Self and the material modifications of my own body that it is impossible to doubt that destruction of the body implies dissolution of the Self. With equal certainty we must reject a world existing outside Self, because both consist of the same empirical 'elements', and in fact that to which the term 'world' is applied consists *entirely* of elements which also belong to Self. In any case, that

The problem

to which we give the name 'world' is only a complex within the Self, but my own body is only a complex within the world-complex. Hence what is known as 'world' would be completely eliminated by a destructive attack on one small part of itself—of which, furthermore, it contains millions of examples: a dreadful piece of nonsense!

If on the other hand we start from the world *alone*, this naturally does away with the grounds for supposing that the world ceases with the destruction of one's own body. But there then arises the following paradox, which has up till now only been fully recognised, I think, in Indian Samkhya philosophy:

Assume two human bodies, A and B. Put A in some particular external situation so that some particular image is seen, let us say the view of a garden. At the same time B is placed in a dark room. If A is now put into the dark room and B in the situation in which A was before, there is then no view of the garden: it is completely dark (because A is *my* body, B someone else's!). This is a flagrant contradiction, for there is no more adequate ground for this phenomenon, considered in general and as a whole, than there would be for one side of a symmetrically loaded balance to go down. Of course, this *one* body is different from all the rest in many other respects as well. It is always seen from a very peculiar and quite special angle. It alone is movable at will, or to put this another way—we shall be returning later to an analysis of the will—it is the only one of which certain movements are known in advance, with almost apodictic certainty, in the very moment of their initiation. It is the only one which hurts when injured. We could very well take any one of these peculiarities and think of it as the adequate ground of all the others. But there is no ground for seeing how, amongst *all* bodies, *one* should be distinguished from *all* the others by the *totality* of these characteristics, unless we mentally insert a real perceptible soul-self spatially and materially into the *inside* of that particular body—and this is the naïve conception which we dismissed from the start without even discussing it.

Essentially, it is this same difficulty, seen of course in a quite different light, that we encounter in the following well-known consideration (as indeed a large number of philosophy's real problems, not to say all, converge on this central point).

Consider any sense-perception; for example, that of a particular tree. Many philosophers have affirmed that one must distinguish the perception which a man has of the tree from the tree itself or the tree 'in itself'. The grounds offered for this at a naïve level are that the tree itself certainly does not enter the observer, but only certain effects proceeding from it. Perhaps we can justify this from a rather more advanced point of view, in that nowadays we can state with certainty that the tree is seen and perceived if and only if certain events, quite unknown to us in detail, occur in the observer's central nervous system. However, this much we can say about these events: that if we knew them precisely we would not describe *these events* as a tree, not as the perception of a tree, nor as a perceived tree. Then is it correct to say that we perceive these events—which are the immediate substratum of our feeling and thinking? Surely not, or we would not find ourselves

The problem

in such a deplorable state of hopeless ignorance about them. So *what* do we perceive, or where is this perception-of-a-tree which we are to distinguish from the tree itself?

E. Mach, R. Avenarius, W. Schuppe and others have, as we know, found a very simple and radical way out of *this* difficulty, which runs somewhat as follows. Kant having established that the 'tree in itself' is not only (as the English philosophers knew already) colourless, odourless, tasteless, and so on, but also belongs entirely to the realm of things-in-themselves which must in absolutely every respect remain inaccessible to our experience, we are in a position to declare once and for all that this thing-in-itself holds no interest for us whatever; that we are going, if necessary, to *disregard* it. Now, in the realm of things which *do* interest us, the tree presents itself just *once*, and we can just as well call this *single* datum a tree as a perception-of-a-tree—the first having the advantage of brevity. This *one* tree, then, is the one datum we have: it is at one and the same time the tree of physics and the tree of psychology. As we observed at an earlier point, the *same* elements go to make up both the Self and the external world, and in various complex forms are sometimes described as constituents of the external world—things—and sometimes as constituents of the Self—sensations, perceptions. These thinkers call this the restoration of the natural concept of the world, or the vindication of naïve realism. It does away with a whole mass of pseudo-problems, in particular the famous *ignorabimus* of Du Bois Reymond, of how feeling and consciousness could arise from a movement of atoms.

Seek for the Road

But what if I am standing in front of that tree, not alone but with some of my fellow human beings, and that I realise, being adequately assured of this by means of communication, that we all perceive the tree in the same way? I then have to suppose that what is numerically *one* complex of elements—the tree—is simultaneously a constituent of several consciousnesses, that it belongs simultaneously to several selves, that it is held *in common*. Not, note, that it is a common *object* of perception, but that it is a *common constituent of perception*. And in fact none of the thinkers named above has shrunk from this—at first sight—somewhat curious conclusion. Mach, for instance, has said (*Analyse der Empfindungen*, 3rd ed., p. 274) that he draws 'no essential distinction between my sensations and someone else's. *The same elements* [his italics] cohere at a number of points of combination, which are selves.' Avenarius and, with particular emphasis, Schuppe, express themselves in the same sense. Thus Schuppe says (in Avenarius, *Der menschliche Weltbegriff*, 3rd ed., p. 155): 'What I am most anxious to emphasise continually is that, while a good deal of the content of consciousness is in this sense subjective, not all of it is; rather, a part of the contents of the consciousness of various selves is not merely qualitatively similar but is and must be their common content, being numerically one and the same, being in the strict sense common to them.'

This conclusion, though it is the only logical one, immediately strikes us westerners as thoroughly bizarre. We are too far removed from what Mach and Avenarius call naïve realism, and have accustomed ourselves to thinking (though there is nothing to prove it, and the

The problem

most primitive daily experience demonstrates the contrary) that each person's sensation, perception and thought is a strictly segregated sphere, these spheres having nothing in common with each other, neither overlapping nor directly influencing each other, but on the contrary absolutely excluding each other. In my opinion, the idea of elements of consciousness which are quite simply common to several human individuals is, in itself, neither self-contradictory nor in contradiction with other known facts of experience; rather, it does very properly restore that state of things which in fact exists for a really naïve human being. And it would be much too narrow to ascribe this common existence only to those 'sense-perceptions' which are 'induced' in various persons by the 'external object'. Shared thoughts, with several people really thinking the same thing—which happens far more often in practical life than, say, in science—really are thoughts in common, and they are *single* occurrences; any numerical statement about how many of them there are, based on a count of the number of individuals engaged in thinking, is quite without meaning in respect of what is being thought.

The first real paradox confronts us at the same point at which we left it further back. The idea of largely common elements cohering in a number of points, which are selves, is clear and good so long as we eliminate ourselves, our own really special Self, and remain non-participating external describers of the whole situation, like a sort of extra-mundane god. But as soon as I remember that I am one of these selves myself, that this whole structure of elements presents itself, constantly and unremittingly, in just one highly unsymmetrical and arbitrary perspective and in no other, then I have to ask what it is that thus distinguishes this *one* point in the whole, and so on, leading to exactly the same argument as we had before.

V

THE VEDANTIC VISION

And thy spirit's highest fiery flight
Is satisfied with likeness and with image.
GOETHE

For philosophy, then, the real difficulty lies in the spatial and temporal multiplicity of observing and thinking individuals. If all events took place in *one* consciousness, the whole situation would be extremely simple. There would then be something given, a simple datum, and this, however otherwise constituted, could scarcely present us with a difficulty of such magnitude as the one we do in fact have on our hands.

I do not think that this difficulty can be logically resolved, by consistent thought, within our intellects. But it is quite easy to express the solution in words, thus: the plurality that we perceive is only *an appearance*; *it is not real*. Vedantic philosophy, in which this is a fundamental dogma, has sought to clarify it by a number of analogies, one of the most attractive being the many-faceted crystal which, while showing hundreds of little pictures of what is in reality a single existent object, does

The Vedantic vision

not really multiply that object. We intellectuals of today are not accustomed to admit a pictorial analogy as a philosophical insight; we insist on logical deduction. But, as against this, it may perhaps be possible for logical thinking to disclose at least this much: that to grasp the basis of phenomena through logical thought may in all probability be impossible, since logical thought is itself a part of phenomena, and wholly involved in them; and we may ask ourselves whether, in that case, we are obliged to deny ourselves the use of an allegoric picture of the situation, merely on the grounds that its fitness cannot be strictly proved. In a considerable number of cases logical thinking brings us up to a certain point and then leaves us in the lurch. Faced with an area not directly accessible to these lines of thought but one into which they seem to lead, we may manage to fill it in in such a way that the lines do not simply peter out, but converge on some central point in that area; this may amount to an extremely valuable rounding-out of our picture of the world, and its worth is not to be judged by those standards of rigorous, unequivocal inescapability from which we started out. There are hundreds of cases in which science uses this procedure, and it has long been recognised as justified.

Later on we shall try to adduce some support for the basic Vedantic vision, chiefly by pointing out particular lines in modern thought which converge upon it. Let us first be permitted to sketch a concrete picture of an *experience* which may lead towards it. In what follows, the particular situation described at the beginning could be replaced, equally fittingly, by any other; it is merely meant as a reminder that this is something that needs to be *experienced*, not simply given a notional acknowledgement.

Suppose you are sitting on a bench beside a path in high mountain country. There are grassy slopes all around, with rocks thrusting through them; on the opposite slope of the valley there is a stretch of scree with a low growth of alder bushes. Woods climb steeply on both sides of the valley, up to the line of treeless pasture; and facing you, soaring up from the depths of the valley, is the mighty, glacier-tipped peak, its smooth snowfields and hard-edged rock-faces touched at this moment with soft rose-colour by the last rays of the departing sun, all marvellously sharp against the clear, pale, transparent blue of the sky.

According to our usual way of looking at it, everything that you are seeing has, apart from small changes, been there for thousands of years before you. After a while—not long—you will no longer exist, and the woods and rocks and sky will continue, unchanged, for thousands of years after you.

What is it that has called you so suddenly out of nothingness to enjoy for a brief while a spectacle which remains quite indifferent to you? The conditions for your existence are almost as old as the rocks. For thousands of years men have striven and suffered and begotten and women have brought forth in pain. A hundred years ago, perhaps, another man sat on this spot; like you he gazed with awe and yearning in his heart at the dying light on the glaciers. Like you he was begotten of man and born of woman. He felt pain and brief joy as you do. *Was* he someone else? Was it not you yourself? What is this Self of yours? What was the

The Vedantic vision

necessary condition for making the thing conceived this time into *you*, just *you* and not someone else? What clearly intelligible *scientific* meaning can this 'someone else' really have? If she who is now your mother had cohabited with someone else and had a son by him, and your father had done likewise, would *you* have come to be? Or were you living in them, and in your father's father...thousands of years ago? And even if this is so, why are you not your brother, why is your brother not you, why are you not one of your distant cousins? What justifies you in obstinately discovering this difference—the difference between you and someone else—when objectively what is there is *the same*?

Looking and thinking in that manner you may suddenly come to see, in a flash, the profound rightness of the basic conviction in Vedanta: it is not possible that this unity of knowledge, feeling and choice which you call *your own* should have sprung into being from nothingness at a given moment not so long ago; rather this knowledge, feeling and choice are essentially eternal and unchangeable and numerically *one* in all men, nay in all sensitive beings. But not in *this* sense—that *you* are a part, a piece, of an eternal, infinite being, an aspect or modification of it, as in Spinoza's pantheism. For we should then have the same baffling question: which part, which aspect are *you*? what, objectively, differentiates it from the others? No, but, inconceivable as it seems to ordinary reason, you—and all other conscious beings as such—are all in all. Hence this life of yours which you are living is not merely a piece of the entire existence, but is in a certain sense the *whole*; only this whole is not so constituted that it can be surveyed in one single glance. This, as we know, is what the Brahmins express in that sacred, mystic formula which is yet really so simple and so clear: *Tat tvam asi*, this is you. Or, again, in such words as 'I am in the east and in the west, I am below and above, *I am this whole world*'.

Thus you can throw yourself flat on the ground, stretched out upon Mother Earth, with the certain conviction that you are one with her and she with you. You are as firmly established, as invulnerable as she, indeed a thousand times firmer and more invulnerable. As surely as she will engulf you tomorrow, so surely will she bring you forth anew to new striving and suffering. And not merely 'some day': now, today, every day she is bringing you forth, not *once* but thousands upon thousands of times, just as every day she engulfs you a thousand times over. For eternally and always there is only *now*, one and the same now; the present is the only thing that has no end.

It is the vision of this truth (of which the individual is seldom conscious in his actions) which underlies all morally valuable activity. It brings a man of nobility not only to risk his life for an end which he recognises or believes to be good but—in rare cases—to lay it down in full serenity, even when there is no prospect of saving his own person. It guides the hand of the well-doer—this perhaps even more rarely—when, without hope of future reward, he gives to relieve a stranger's suffering what he cannot spare without suffering himself.

VI

AN EXOTERIC INTRODUCTION TO SCIENTIFIC THOUGHT

There is one idea included, if only partially expressed and exoteric in character, in that fundamental vision we have been discussing, which modern scientific thought might well find relatively little difficulty in assimilating: namely, that the acts of propagation by which a series of genetically connected individuals proceed one from another are not really an interruption but only a constriction of both bodily and spiritual life. Thus we can speak of the identity of an individual's consciousness with that of one of his ancestors in much the same sense as we can of the identity of my consciousness before and after a deep sleep. The usual argument against recognition of this fact is to point to the presence of memory in the one case and its ostensibly complete absence in the other. But today the recognition has surely, to a large extent, won through that, at least in the *instincts* of many animals, we are confronted by nothing less than supra-individual memory. Well-known examples include: the building of nests by birds, when the nest often exactly fits the size and number of eggs to be expected in this particular species, though there is no possibility of individual experience of this; then there is the 'bed-making' observed in many dogs, stamping down the grass of the steppes on the Persian carpet; and the efforts of cats to bury their excreta, even on wooden or stone floors, which obviously makes sense as a precaution against being smelt by an enemy or quarry.

The discovery of similar phenomena in man is made difficult by the fact that there is always an interior awareness of one's action, combined with the conviction —mistaken, in my opinion—that actions are only to be described as instinctive if they take place entirely without thought, without any accompanying deliberation. Hence there is a strong inclination to cast doubt on the description of such a thing as a *memory* of the species, with its stress on the subjective side of the matter, and to reject the whole group of phenomena as having no evidential value for that idea of continuity which we are talking about. Yet there is one complex in man, as in animals, which has a strong emotional colouring, and bears the unmistakable mark of supra-individual memory: the first awakening of sexual feeling, the feelings of attraction and repulsion between the sexes, sexual curiosity, sexual shame, and so on. The whole of that hardly describable, partly painful, partly heavenly emotion, and in particular its obstinately selective character when we fall in love, which most clearly indicates special memory traces in the individual, which are not common to the entire species.

I can see another example of 'ekphoria' (Semon's word) of a primitive inherited engram in a group of phenomena occurring in some people in everyday life in connection with what is called 'having a row'. Someone infringes our rights (whether in actual fact or in our opinion), and at once we feel moved or impelled to energetic reaction, reprimand, abuse, or something of the sort. We get 'worked up', the pulse-rate increases,

An exoteric introduction

blood rushes to the head, the muscles tense up, tremble, become 'charged' as it were, and are often irresistibly impelled to go into action. In short, the whole organism visibly prepares in an admirable fashion for what thousands of our ancestors in similar circumstances actually *did*: for physical attack or defence against the aggressor, which in *their* case was the right and requisite thing to do. For us, it usually is not. Nevertheless, we have no control over this set of phenomena; they occur in anyone who is inclined that way, even if he knows perfectly well that any actual violence on his part is quite out of the question or would cause him grievous harm, so that he would never seriously consider it for a moment; and, in particular, even when his conscious will is exclusively and intensively directed at conducting an effective defence in *words*, because (I will suppose) these alone can protect him from serious harm, as could his ancestors' fists in *their* case. This means that the whole atavistic mechanism of tension gravely hampers the use of his own means of defence. The *mnemic* character (in Semon's sense) of the phenomenon is further indicated in a very clear way by the efforts of the organism to overcome this 'incongruence in mnemic homophony'. The continuation of the engram-series is 'Hit out'. In reality we usually have to control ourselves and don't we know how painful an effort it is! And how vigorously the mnemic law makes itself felt when for once, in defiance of reason, we act in accordance with it. The common-sense way of judging such behaviour is, by the way, entirely in accordance with our interpretation. There is the sense of facing an elemental force of nature; indeed, the man who is behaving in this way often

Seek for the Road

knows, himself, that he is doing something for which he has no real motive, and that he is not being guided by motive in the ordinary sense and will therefore perhaps be feeling remorseful the next moment.

These are special cases in which the intrusion of ancestral events, the effective influence of an earlier layer in our being, not formed during our own individual life, is especially noticeable. They could be multiplied still further, with a greater or less degree of certainty: I think in particular of 'sympathy' and 'antipathy'; of loathing aroused by certain harmless animals; of the sense of being at home in some locality, and so on. But these are not the only kind of examples of what we mean by asserting the continuity or identity of consciousness; we would still assert it even if we had no such cases to point to by way of illustration.

My conscious life depends on a particular constitution and way of functioning on the part of my soma, and especially of my central nervous system. But these are in direct causal and genetic dependence on the structure and way of functioning of earlier somata, all likewise associated with conscious mental life, and there has been no interruption at any point in the series of physiological events; on the contrary, each of these bodies was at the same time blueprint, builder and material for the next one, so that a part of it grew into a copy of itself. Where in all this are we to place the beginning of a new consciousness?

But the special constitution and the formed habits of my brain, my individual experience, in fact, all that I really call my personality—surely *these* are not predetermined by what happened to my ancestors! If by

An exoteric introduction

this last I mean only my individual series of ancestors, then indeed not. This brings us to the point at which we have to consider very carefully the scope of that *partial* statement with which we began this chapter. For the structure of what I call my higher spiritual self is indeed essentially the direct consequence of ancestral events, but not exclusively nor principally within the limits of my physical ancestors. If what follows is to seem anything more than a bold piece of rhetorical trickery, it is necessary to be clear on one point concerning the two factors which determine an individual's course of development, namely (*a*) the special arrangement of his genes, and (*b*) the special pattern of the environment which works on him; it is necessary, I say, to realise that these two factors are of quite the same nature, in that the special arrangement of the genes, with all the possibilities of development which it contains, has developed under the influence of and in essential dependence upon earlier environments. And now consider how totally the emergence of the spiritual personality is bound up with environmental influences which are the direct outcome of the spiritual personalities of other members of the species, some living, some dead. And always remember that we scientists may and indeed must regard all these 'spiritual' influences as direct modifications of our individual soma (that is, the cerebral system) by the soma of other individuals, so that there is in principle no difference between *these* influences and those resulting from the succession of physical ancestors.

No Self stands alone. Behind it stretches an immense chain of physical and—as a special class within the whole—mental events, to which it belongs as a reacting member and which it carries on. Through the condition at any moment of its somatic, especially its cerebral, system, *and* through education, and tradition, by word, by writing, by monument, by manners, by a way of life, by a newly shaped environment...by so much that a thousand words would not exhaust it, by all that, I say, the Self is not so much *linked* with what happened to its ancestors, it is not so much the product, and merely the product, of all that, but rather, in the strictest sense of the word, the SAME THING as all that: the strict, direct continuation of it, just as the Self aged fifty is the continuation of the Self aged forty.

It is rather remarkable that whereas western philosophy has almost universally accepted the idea that the death of the individual does not put an end to anything that is of the essence of life, it has (with the exception of Plato and Schopenhauer) bestowed hardly a thought on this other idea, much deeper and more intimately joyful, which logically goes almost hand in hand with it: the idea that the same thing applies to individual *birth*, at which what happens is not that I am created for the first time but that I slowly awaken as though from a deep sleep. Then I can see my hopes and strivings, my fears and cares as the *same* as those of thousands who have lived before me, and I may hope that future centuries may bring fulfilment to my yearnings of centuries ago. No seed of thought can germinate in me except as the continuation of some forebear; not really a new seed but the predetermined unfolding of a bud on the ancient, sacred tree of life.

I know very well that most of my readers, despite

An exoteric introduction

Schopenhauer and the Upanishads, while perhaps admitting the validity of what is said here as a pleasing and appropriate metaphor, will withhold their agreement from any *literal* application of the proposition that all consciousness is essentially *one*. Even the thesis that consciousness is identical within the family tree will have been countered with the numerical fact that, generally speaking, *two* parents produce *several* children and continue to live thereafter. Further, the extinction of all special experience in the child will seem too total to justify any assertion of continuity. To me, this logical-arithmetical contradiction involved in the family tree is a positive reassurance, because it seems to me that *this* is precisely the point at which the assertion of identity is in fact scientifically proved, and hence that the contradiction loses its force also in relation to the Vedantic thesis as a whole, or at least that the applicability of arithmetic to these things becomes extremely dubious. As for the very thorough extinction of memory (which is surely for many people, in their heart of hearts, the fishiest part of this physiological mock-immortality!): even apart from any metaphysical view, we may consider how well adapted this recurrent smoothing-out of the impressionable wax is for the formation of *this thing* which, even if it does not, as Schopenhauer thought, *want* to be formed, nevertheless in fact *is* being formed.

VII
MORE ABOUT NON-PLURALITY

If you divide the little fresh-water polyp *Hydra fusca* in two, even if you do it very unsymmetrically so that one part gets all the tentacles and the other part none, *both* parts will develop into complete, slightly smaller specimens of *Hydra*; and that game can be played repeatedly (Verworn, *Allgemeine Physiologie*, chap. 1; Fischer: Jena, 1915). This is by no means a unique case amongst organisms at this level; R. Semon (*Mneme*, 2nd ed., p. 151) reports the same thing of *Planaria*, amongst others. His special interest in the matter is that he sees this reproduction of the missing part, not unreasonably, as strictly analogous to associative reproduction in the higher kinds of memory. In the same way Semon sees the recapitulation of the whole evolutionary process, which regularly takes place in the higher animals and plants from the embryonic stage upwards, as parallel to the recapitulation of a poem learnt by heart: and this not as a metaphor, but in the real sense that both phenomena are to be subsumed under the higher concept for which he uses the word 'mnemic'. But the whole of this idea and the grounds for it can be read in Semon's own works (*Mneme* and *Mnemische Empfindungen*); I will say no more here than that, while it seems to appeal very little to Semon's narrower fellow-specialists, it has been applauded with the utmost enthusiasm by A. Forel, who, being equally eminent as a psychiatrist

More about non-plurality

and as a zoologist, seems equipped, as few others are, to pass judgement on the fitness of the parallel.

The reason why I have introduced this division experiment at this point is as follows. I want the reader to think himself into *Hydra fusca*. We cannot but attribute *some kind of consciousness*, however dim and undifferentiated, to our primitive little cousin on the ladder of life. And this consciousness will appear in both sections as the *undivided* continuation of what was there before. This cannot be logically proved, but we can *feel* that any other notion would be meaningless. To divide or multiply consciousness is something meaningless. In all the world, there is no kind of framework within which we can find consciousness in the plural; this is simply something we construct because of the spatio-temporal plurality of individuals, but it is a false construction. Because of it, all philosophy succumbs again and again to the hopeless conflict between the theoretically unavoidable acceptance of Berkeleian idealism and its complete uselessness for understanding the real world. The only solution to this conflict, in so far as any is available to us at all, lies in the ancient wisdom of the Upanishads.

If consciousness were not a metaphysical *singulare tantum*, it would be difficult to see why plurality does not become manifest even within the framework of one human consciousness, since the description of our soma or even of our nervous system as a single individual is highly problematical. Our soma is a city of cells and organs, within which there are some members with a relatively high degree of independence, such as the blood-corpuscles, the spermatozoa and, in a somewhat different sense, the individual ganglia of the spinal cord. A glance at the rest of the world of organisms tells us that, concerning the degree of self-subsistence in the various parts constituting the one city, every conceivable intermediate form is to be found, in continuous sequence. We find complete interdependence of the members in the higher animals and plants, but with this difference: in animal bodies, because of the type of specialisation that they have achieved, separation of any considerable part leads with certainty to the death of one part and in many cases of both; whereas with plants, conditions being suitable, both parts can continue to live. At the other extreme we find animal 'states' consisting of single individuals not spatially combined, with a relatively high degree of independence in the members—cities of ants, termites, bees and men. But between the two extremes there are, as we have said, numerous intermediate members of the series, and it would be a great mistake to understand the word 'city' or 'state' as applied to all these cases merely in the sense of a metaphor or analogy. A man or an ant will not survive if he *really* gets separated from the (biological) unity of the state and left on his own, and this for the very same reason that a single cell or organ of a higher animal will die if separated from the unity of the organism: because specialisation has proceeded too far, and the separated fragment, out of contact with the rest of the organism, is deprived of the environmental conditions which it needs. If these environmental conditions are supplied, even a separate organ can go on living, as grafting experiments have shown.

More about non-plurality

For intermediate forms, we can point both to 'divisible' organisms like *Hydra* and *Planaria* and to the many lower organisms in which division—forming of colonies—is the normal mode of reproduction. Verworn (*loc. cit.* p. 68) gives a particularly interesting example: *Siphonophora*, a group of *coelenterata*. These organisms consist of a collection of relatively strongly differentiated organs, some of which are for locomotion, some for feeding, some for reproduction and others for the protection of the body as a whole. But these organs are still self-subsistent to such a degree that some of them, for example the swimming-bells, are capable in certain cases of breaking loose from the parent and leading an independent existence as *medusae*.

This glance, for purposes of comparison, at the organic kingdom teaches us what we really are somatically: a cell-state, united, delimited and indivisible only in a very limited sense. If I try to hold on to the currently predominant view and derive the unity of my Self, of which my experience makes me extremely certain, from the superficial, relative unity of a somatic individual, I find myself faced with an impenetrable thicket of questions, each branded only too clearly with the marks of a pseudo-problem. Why is it precisely at this *intermediate level* in the hierarchy of successively superimposed unities (cell, organ, human body, state)—why, I ask, is it precisely at the level of my body that unitary self-consciousness comes into the picture, whereas the cell and the organ do not as yet possess it and the state possesses it no longer? Or, if this is not so, how is my Self constituted out of the individual selves of my brain-cells? Is there a higher Self similarly constituted out of the consciousness of myself and my fellow-men, equally and directly conscious of itself as a unity—the Self of the state or of the whole of humanity? Some very distinguished minds have felt the compulsion of fantasies of this kind; I will name only Theodor Fechner. They are almost unavoidable so long as one continues to see the unity of the Self as based on the unity of the soma, after having come to see how relative and problematical this latter unity is. Such questions vanish as soon as the root of that directly experienced unity which leads to the hypothesis of the Self is transferred to the metaphysical unity, the essential uniqueness of consciousness in general. The categories of *number*, of *whole* and of *parts* are then simply not applicable to it; the most adequate, though no doubt still somewhat mystical expression of the situation being this: the self-consciousness of the individual members are numerically identical both with each other and with that Self which they may be said to form at a higher level; each member is in a certain sense justified in saying '*L'État, c'est moi*'.

The best way to overcome one's resistance to this idea is to keep reminding oneself that it does really rest on direct experience, inasmuch as we never in fact have any experience anywhere of a plurality of consciousness but always and everywhere only of consciousness in the singular. This is the one and only perfectly certain piece of knowledge, to which we can attain without any far-reaching metaphysical hypotheses. Berkeleian idealism sticks to it and is thus consistent and free from contradictions. I can get beyond it only by observing the large number of bodies which are

More about non-plurality

entirely similar in structure to my own body, and which have the same mutual physical interaction with their environment, with each other and with my body as the latter has with its environment and with them; and by the hypothesis connected with this observation, namely that these similar physical events may be linked to the same sensations as take place when such events affect my own body. 'There's another one like you sitting over there, thinking and feeling go on in him too.' And now everything depends on how we go on: whether with 'I am over there too, Self is over there, that is myself'; or with 'There is a self over there, like yours, a second one'. It is the word 'a' which differentiates the two ideas, the indefinite article, degrading 'self' to a common noun. It is only this 'a' which makes the breach with idealism irreparable, fills the world with ghosts and drives us helplessly into the arms of animism.

To be sure, anything that my friend A tells me of what he is at this moment feeling, perceiving or thinking is *not* an immediate content of my consciousness. But neither am I directly conscious of what I myself felt, perceived or thought an hour ago or a year ago. I can only find more or less clear traces of it, hardly different in any essential way from those which A's communication induces in me in respect of *his* feelings, etc. It also happens that, when attention alternates regularly between two separate fields of ideas, long continuous chains can exist side by side in the same intellect, almost without contact with each other. If contact is established (which not infrequently leads to important new insights) what happens then bears a very strong resemblance to a lively interchange of ideas between two different individuals. Conversely, close intellectual collaboration between two men can bring about to an incredible degree a fusing of their spheres of consciousness in an empirical unity.

Wishing to refute the identity of individual consciousnesses, one might make use of the following crude thought-experiment. I construct twenty different arithmetical examples, each so tiresome that a bright schoolboy would need only just under an hour to work it. Then I put twenty capable pupils in a classroom and get them each to work one of my sums between ten and eleven o'clock on such-and-such a day. At ten o'clock none of them knew what his problem was to be, at eleven they are all finished. *One* consciousness could not have done it, which proves the numerical plurality of consciousness.

As against this we must point out that these 'twenty acts of consciousness' certainly *cannot* be simply added together or summed up as a 'twenty-fold power', as could, say, the power of a number of dynamos. They cannot be 'put in series'; assuming exactly equal ability in all of them, they cannot achieve more in combination, in the sense of solving a more difficult problem, than any one of them alone; not, that is, unless, in the course of discussion, consultation and exploration, some development takes place in their capabilities—which will then happen to all of them equally. Thus, conversely, each individual member of the team would have been capable of solving all twenty problems, though he would have taken somewhat longer over it.

More about non-plurality

Nor can one say that the suffering of twenty or a thousand mothers who lose their sons in a single battle is twenty or a thousand times that of one single mother thus afflicted. Nor is the pleasure enjoyed when twenty or a thousand young men sleep with their girls twenty or a thousand times as great as when this only happens in a single case. And yet these events of consciousness are perfectly capable of being heightened and so to speak multiplied, as when for example a mother suffers the pain of seeing *both* her sons killed.

If, finally, we look back at that idea of Mach, Avenarius and Schuppe which we outlined earlier on, we shall realise that it comes as near to the orthodox dogma of the Upanishads as it could possibly do without stating it *expressis verbis*. The external world and consciousness are one and the same thing, in so far as both are constituted by the same primitive elements. But we are then hardly even using a different formula whether we express the essential *community* of these elements in all individuals by saying that there is only *one* external world or that there is only *one* consciousness.

VIII
CONSCIOUSNESS, ORGANIC, INORGANIC, MNEME

Whatever philosophical position we adopt, it is a practically indubitable fact of experience that the manifestation of a higher kind of intellectual life is bound up with the functioning of a highly developed brain. The world that we construct out of our sensations and perceptions, and which we always comfortably think of as being quite simply *there*, is not in fact manifest just by existing; in order to be so, it requires very special events in very special parts of itself, namely the functions of a brain. This is an extraordinarily remarkable state of affairs, in view of which one cannot help asking, however tentatively, what are the special distinguishing characteristics of events in the brain, by which they and they alone bring about this manifestation; is it possible to state, or at least to conjecture, which material events have this capacity, and which have not? Or, more simply, and perhaps just as unambiguously, which material events are directly connected with consciousness?

For the present-day thinker with a rational-scientific outlook there is a quick and obvious answer to this question: to judge by our own experience and the analogy provided by the higher animals, consciousness is associated exclusively with a certain type of event in organic, living matter, that is, with certain nerve functions. As to how far down the ranks of animals we can

Consciousness and mneme

suppose that consciousness extends, and as to how it is constituted in its earliest stages, the search for more definite ideas on this subject would set us an insoluble and superfluous task which—we are told—we may well leave to dreamers with nothing better to do. It would be even more idle and fantastic to consider whether altogether different events, even inorganic events, or even all events whatsoever, might be associated with some kind of consciousness; this is dismissed as pure fantasy, in which everyone can please himself as to what he supposes, certain only that such suppositions do not contribute anything to knowledge.

There is no denying the justice of this view; yet I do not think that those who are content with it are always completely clear about the monstrous gap which it leaves unfilled in our picture of the world, otherwise they would not be so cheerfully satisfied with it. Though it may perhaps be the case that organic, living existence is more universal than inorganic (about which we shall say more later on), nevertheless the appearance of nerve tissue and brains is a very special occurrence within the organic realm, and an occurrence whose significance and importance is fairly clear to us. We can state the part played by the mechanism of the brain within spatio-temporal events while leaving entirely out of account the peculiar way in which it is bound up with sensation. That is to say, it is, without any doubt whatever, a quite special form of adaptive mechanism which has arisen in the course of the struggle for existence, whether by natural selection or in some other way; its effect is that its possessor constantly reacts to his variable environment in a way favourable to him-

Seek for the Road

self and hence to the survival of his species. It is certainly the most complicated and ingenious of all such mechanisms, and where it is present it usually assumes outstanding importance, a position of dominance, in the true sense of the word, over the whole soma. But it is not the only mechanism of that kind, and there are large groups of organisms which do not possess it.

And then, on the other hand, we say that consciousness is that by which this world first becomes manifest, by which indeed, we can quite calmly say, it first becomes present; that the world *consists* of the elements of consciousness—this world *within* which we have just discovered the emergence of the brain as a highly specialised phenomenon, something which has emerged but which might quite well have remained non-existent and which is, in any case, by no means *sui generis*. And now we are asked to believe that this special modification in the evolution of the higher mammals had to happen in order that the world should dawn on itself in the light of consciousness; whereas, if it had not emerged, this world would have remained nothing but a drama played to an empty house, not present *to* anyone and hence not in the real sense present at all! If this is really the ultimate wisdom to which we can attain in this question, then to me it seems to be the utter bankruptcy of our picture of the world. And we ought at least to acknowledge it, and not act as though it did not matter to us, or jeer, in our rationalistic wisdom, at those who try to find a way out, however desperate.

There is something far grander, far more in accord with a clear recognition of what it is all about, in the

Consciousness and mneme

ideas of Spinoza or Fechner. For Spinoza, the human body is 'a modification of the infinite substance (God), in so far as it is expressed in the attribute of extension', and the human mind is *that same* modification, but expressed in the attribute of thought. But since according to him every material thing is a modification of God in this way and, as such, expresses both these attributes, this, when translated into our language, means nothing else than: that something corresponds to every material event in the way that our consciousness corresponds to the vital processes of our body. And Fechner's fertile mind went on to imagine not only plants but also the planet Earth and the stars as possessed of souls. I do not agree with these fantasies, but I would prefer not to have to pass judgement on the question of which came nearer to the ultimate truth, Fechner or the bankrupts of modern rationalism.

In the next chapter I shall be making some remarks which may perhaps help to achieve a small step forward in this matter. First, I want to introduce here a brief discussion—as I promised you before—on the relation of organic to inorganic.

To begin with a purely factual statement: inorganic matter—the subject-matter, by definition, of physics and chemistry—is an abstraction which, unless by special arrangement, we actually encounter scarcely anywhere, or at any rate extremely seldom. If we consider our earthly environment, it consists almost exclusively of the living or dead bodies of plants and animals. This is certain as regards a great part of the earth's crust. Hence one might well feel tempted to doubt the accuracy of the common view that everything starts from the inorganic, with the organic only a special modification of the inorganic, and wonder whether it is standing the actual situation on its head. 'But we know what organisms are, we know the conditions in which they can live, and we can conclude from this that the situation on most of the bodies in the universe is exactly the reverse.' Yes, indeed, we know *our* world of organisms, we know that *its* living tissue is compounded in a very special way of a relatively small number of elements. But would it not be much more natural to explain this fact by the very special and relatively constant conditions of this environment, and to suppose that other environmental conditions would bring forth some other form of organic existence?

The question then certainly arises: What does 'organic' mean?—that is, in the wider sense here supposed, naturally excluding such simple answers as 'protein' or 'protoplasm'. Fixing our attention on a somewhat wider concept than this, we arrive at the criterion of *metabolism*. Thus Schopenhauer's line of demarcation may be regarded as highly suitable, when he says that in inorganic being 'the essential and permanent element, the basis of identity and integrity, is the material, the *matter*, the inessential and mutable element being the form. In organic being the reverse is true; for its life, that is, its existence as an organic being, consists precisely in a constant change of matter while the form persists.'

But it depends entirely on the observer what he chooses to regard as essential and what as inessential in a thing. *Per se* everything is equally essential. This would turn 'organic' and 'inorganic' into characteristics, not so much of the object as of our point of view or the

Consciousness and mneme

direction of our attention. And this is true. If we are following the course of an atom, it makes no difference to it whether or not its path leads it through a living organism. We are then dealing only with physical interactions, and we are convinced that physics suffices, in principle, to answer all the questions that may arise. On the other hand it strikes us as strange, at least at first sight, that we should have the right to regard—for example—the propagation of changes of state within a medium, such as a volcanic eruption or a flowing river as it changes down the centuries, or a glacier, or a flame, as even the roughest and crudest forms of organic being. But despite such offences against current usage, it seems to me that the idea that the *fundamental* contrast between organic and inorganic lies not in the constitution of the object but in the attitude of the observer is well worth considering. It does away with that recurrent doubt whether it is conceivable that organic being, which is 'so utterly different', could have 'gradually' emerged from the inorganic. In fact, though there is perfect continuity in the object, the transition is *not* gradual; because the mental focus can only change abruptly, even though the structure of the object exerts increasing pressure on it to change gradually. I can *either* focus my observation on the unchanging material with its changing form, *or* on the unchanging form of this changing matter, but not very well on both at once. In the same way, I can express the equations of hydrodynamics either in Lagrange's form or Euler's; both forms have exactly the same content, yet cannot emerge from each other gradually but only by means of the single discontinuous step of changing the variables.

Seek for the Road

Of course this realisation will not hinder us, but on the contrary spur us on to search for the mechanism which gives specialised organic tissue, in the narrower sense, its characteristic stamp. It is the peculiarity which Semon calls *mneme*, by which a particular reaction, set in motion once, or more than once, by some stimulus-complex, gets 'drilled in' in such a way that in later, similar occurrences, only a part, and often a very small part, of the original stimulus-complex is needed in order to achieve the same result. The mechanism of this process is still completely unknown; furthermore, there is as yet absolutely no mechanical model which would illustrate the process even in the quite general sense in which Boltzmann's bicycle model illustrates electro-magnetic processes; whereas we do have, in the physical action of a *relay*, a very effective illustration, at least in this sense, for the peculiar character of *stimulation* itself.[1] Of course, no one has yet given very serious thought to the possibility of constructing a model of this sort for mneme,[2] important though it would be for the advancement of our knowledge.

---

[1] The peculiar thing about reaction to a stimulus, unlike ordinary physical reactions, is that there is no simple ratio of cause to effect. Effects take place which cannot be immediately understood in terms of the external structure of the systems which are reacting, but which have to be linked up with the internal structure, not discernible from the outside, of at least one of the systems. A relay has all these features too.

[2] Semon calls for this to be done when he says (*Mneme*, 2nd ed., p. 385): 'We need of course to have physicists and chemists working and researching towards the same goal from the other end, to find out whether, and how far, it is possible to discern something corresponding to engraphy and ekphoria at the inorganic level. Up till now we have nothing usable of this sort.'

IX
ON BECOMING CONSCIOUS

We will now return to the question asked at the beginning of the last chapter—'Which material events are directly associated with consciousness?'—but starting this time from the somewhat surer ground of inner experience. We first tried to show, on general grounds, that the idea that this association is a unique prerogative of the functions of the brain is not very probable; and we then had to admit that attempts at *extending* the association to other events unfortunately lose themselves in vague, fantastic speculations. We now propose to make an observation of an opposite kind, but equally capable of shattering this idea. It runs as follows:

Not all brain-processes are accompanied by consciousness. There are nerve-processes which, while exactly resembling the 'conscious' processes of the brain both in their whole centripetal-centrifugal pattern and in their biological significance as reaction-regulators, nevertheless are not associated with consciousness. They include not only the regulatory reflex processes in the ganglia of the spinal cord and that part of the nervous system which they control, but also a considerable number of reflex events which involve the brain itself but do not enter into consciousness.

So here we have various specimens of very similar nerve-processes taking place within our soma, some of which are accompanied by consciousness and some not;

moreover—and this is something extremely valuable for our analysis—they include intermediate forms at every level. Surely, then, it should not be too difficult to work out the distinguishing characteristic conditions of each by a process of observation and thought!

It seems to me that the key to this lies in the well-known fact that any particular series of phenomena in which we consciously or even actively participate, if it is repeated over and over again in exactly the same way, *gradually sinks out of the sphere of consciousness*; and it is only, so to speak, dragged up into it again if, on a fresh repetition, the event initiating the process, or the conditions affecting its continuance, are slightly different, in which case the reactions happen slightly differently too. But even then it is not the process as a whole, but only (primarily at least) the modifications or differentials, by which the new series is distinguished from the earlier ones, which enter into consciousness.

It is so easy for anyone to supply hundreds of examples of this from his own experience that I can perhaps for the moment spare myself the task of doing so. If I gave one I should have to give a thousand, so as to avoid setting what I mean in too special a light.

In order to appreciate the significance of this gradual fading-out of consciousness in our mental life, we need to realise the enormous part played in it by training through repetition, mneme. Biologically speaking, a single experience is entirely insignificant; only efficient functioning in relation to frequently repeated situations is biologically valuable. And our environment is in fact so constituted that the same or very similar situations do constantly repeat themselves, usually periodically, con-

On becoming conscious

stantly requiring a similar reaction from the organism if it is to maintain itself. We cannot, of course, take these observations back to the beginning; every organism is already, *qua* organism, engraved in millions of ways by its environment. Now let us think of an organism confronted by a new biological situation. It reacts in a certain way and *maintains* itself by doing so, or at any rate is not destroyed. If the stimulus is repeated the same sequence is reproduced, which we will suppose is in the first place of such a nature as to enter into consciousness. Repetition will then introduce something new into consciousness, the element of 'having had this already' (what Avenarius, in the monstrous nomenclature of his criticism of experience, calls 'notal'). But with frequent repetition the performance becomes better and better, as our inner experience shows; it gets less and less 'interesting', the reaction becomes more and more reliable, but also proportionately less and less conscious. Now suppose a change occurs in the external situation. This, or rather the difference in the reaction which it causes, gets through to the consciousness. But again, only so long as it is new. Gradually it too works in and sinks beneath the surface. Nor need the difference consist in a single and thereafter persistent change in the situation and its result; it may and often will be the case that the situation is modified now in one way and now in another, causing the reaction to be modified in a corresponding way. This kind of bifurcation gets worked in too: after a sufficient number of repetitions, the process of deciding in a particular case which situation is happening and how to react to it is performed quite

Seek for the Road

unconsciously. Then a second level of difference can be superimposed on the first, then a third, and so on. And so *ad infinitum*, the only differences which get through to the consciousness being the most recent ones, the ones about which the living tissue is still 'in training'. To give ourselves an *image* of this, we might say that consciousness is the *instructor* supervising the *education* of the living tissue, who is called on for help whenever new problems crop up but leaves the pupils to themselves to deal with those in which he knows they have had sufficient practice.

That is an *image*! I should like to underline *image* twenty times and have it printed in letters covering the whole page. The tendency of our animistic tradition will be, all too surely, to inculcate the idea that when a new situation is encountered, an 'I of consciousness', a little demon, *really is* summoned up to shed light on the situation and take the decision which is then acted on. This notion would be a dreadful misunderstanding, an infernal infantile regression. All we are asserting is the fact that new situations and the new reactions consequent upon them are accompanied by consciousness, and those long since learnt are not.

As I said before, all this can be verified a thousand times over by examples from the sphere of our consciousness as it is today. All the hundreds of little manipulations of daily life had to be learnt, some of them with considerable difficulty; at the time they were most emphatically conscious—we would exult over the first successful performance. Now that we are grown up we tie our shoe-laces, switch on the electric light, take off our clothes in the evening, and so on, without the

On becoming conscious

slightest interruption in our train of thought. The story is told of a certain famous scholar that, having been told by his wife, on an evening when guests were expected, to go to his bedroom and put on a clean collar, he went on mechanically undressing after taking his collar off, got into bed, and switched out the light. This seems quite credible, but only because we can conceive of complete absorption in one's thoughts being combined with completely unconscious action. Or again: suppose that the office to which we have been going every day for years moves elsewhere. We now have to turn off our accustomed road at a certain point. How often, and for how long, shall we be apt to go wrong at that point, and how clearly aware shall we be, at the beginning, of the 'situation-differential' in contrast to the mechanical following of the old route?

It seems to me that it would not be particularly rash to take this feature, which we know so well in the ontogenesis of our mental life, and apply it to its phylogenesis. If we do this, it at once explains the unconscious, reflex character of the functions of the ganglia. They are all concerned with regulating internal reactions, such as peristaltic movements of the intestines and the beating of the heart, which have certainly not for a long time been subject to changes and have been safely learnt and dropped out of the conscious sphere. Breathing is in an intermediate position; it normally takes place in a long-accustomed and completely unconscious way, but in special circumstances, for example, in a smoky atmosphere, it is affected by situation-differentials and reacts in a correspondingly different and conscious way. Hence, according to this view of things, the functions of the ganglia are, so to speak, fixed and fossilised brain-functions.

There is, as we know, one state in which the brain provides us with no more sensation than does a ganglion, namely deep sleep. Now sleep is obviously a time of recuperation for the brain, or rather for those parts of it which, so long as their activity is, so to speak, directed outwards through the open doors of the senses, have to be ready to go into action at any moment and cannot take a rest. It does not immediately appear why this process of recuperation, initiated by a temporary shutting-off of the sensorium, should not be associated for us with some sort of phenomena of consciousness. Evidently this is because, being an interior process long since thoroughly learnt, it no longer undergoes differentiation.

All that has been said so far has referred exclusively to processes of the brain or nerves. But I think that we can now confidently take another step forward without encountering any contradictions. It is a step which will, I know, initially provoke the greatest mistrust; but it is the only one which will bring to a fairly satisfying conclusion, at least in a preliminary sense, our attempt to describe the conditions for the emergence of consciousness.

The whole ontogenesis not only of the brain but of the whole soma is a recapitulation—mnemically well worked in—of events which have taken place thousands of times. Hence there is nothing to prevent us from supposing that what we have so far been asserting as a characteristic of events in the nervous system is a characteristic of organic existence in general: namely, to be associated with consciousness in so far as it is *new*.

On becoming conscious

There is nothing against this supposition; meaning that it is *not* an objection to it that, as we all know of ourselves, ontogenesis takes place unconsciously at first in the womb and for several years of life afterwards, which are chiefly occupied with sleep. The child is then going through a long-established process of development in external conditions which remain relatively constant from one case to another.

It is only the individual peculiarities in any one ontogenesis which become conscious. In so far as an organism possesses organs which function in a constantly adaptive way in relation to the special, changing conditions of its environment, in so far as it is thus influenced, trained and modified by its environment (the modification being such as to become, in the course of generations, fixed as a permanent possession of the species, in the same way as all that has gone before), to this extent organic existence is accompanied by consciousness. We higher vertebrates possess such an organ in the brain, and essentially only in it. So for this reason consciousness in us is associated with events in the brain, because in us the brain is the organ by which we adapt ourselves to changing environmental conditions; it is that part of our soma in which we are engaged in the further evolution of our species; it is, to employ an image, the growth-shoot on our stem.

Briefly summarising, we can express the proposed law thus: consciousness is bound up with *learning* in organic substance; organic *competence* is unconscious. Still more briefly, and put in a form which is admittedly rather obscure and open to misunderstanding: Becoming is conscious, being unconscious.

X
THE MORAL LAW

I freely admit that I would not have been so quick to give my assent to the hypothesis about consciousness which I have been arguing here (the detailed examination of which, if possible at all, I must leave to more informed experts) if I had not observed that it seems to shed a certain amount of light on an area which, while decidedly remote from physiology, is very relevant to us as human beings; and that this gives a certain support to the hypothesis itself. I mean that this opens up the possibility of a scientific interpretation of ethics.

In all ages and amongst all peoples *self-conquest* has formed the underlying basis of all virtue. This appears at once in the fact that a moral *teaching* always appears arrayed as a *demand*, 'Thou shalt'; and it must be so, because if we consider the practical behaviour which we value as morally elevated, positively significant, or wise, the behaviour which, for reasons very variously stated, we applaud, respect or admire, we find that such behaviour, however constituted in detail, always has one thing common to it: a certain opposition to primitive desire.

Whence comes this curious contradiction, interwoven with our entire life, between 'I want' and 'Thou shalt'? It is really highly absurd and unnatural to require always of every individual that he should deny himself, suppress his primitive urges and, in short, be *other* than

The moral law

what he actually *is*. In fact, this is the ground from which in these days (if not in public teaching, yet in the attitude of individuals towards the demands of virtuous living) the most powerful and devastating attacks are being made against all morality (amongst which, by the way, I include the attempt to base it in one form or another on *utility*).

'I am simply as I am. Way, there, for my individuality! Free development for the impulses nature has planted in me! Self-control and self-denial are nonsense and parsonical humbug. God is nature, and nature surely has made me as she sees fit, as I *ought* to be: any other "ought" is bunk.'

This, or something like this, is heard on many sides; at any rate, these maxims, or ones like them, are in fact followed in a great many cases. And one cannot but grant that it seems to have a large measure of justification. The simple, straightforward brutality of this principle, seemingly based on a natural, unforced concept of nature, is hard to refute; Kant's admittedly incomprehensible imperative is powerless against it.

However, its scientific foundation is, we may be thankful to say, unsound. The insight which we have now achieved into the *development* of organisms allows us to understand very well, I think, that our whole life in any case *has to be* and *is* a constant struggle against our primitive self. We shall say something later about 'ought'.

What we call our natural self, our primitive desire with its implanted instincts, is correlated in our consciousness with our *bodily* heritage from our ancestors, what we have *become* phylogenetically up till now. But *we*—meaning those who at any moment can call themselves 'we'—march in the forefront of the generations. We are evolving. In every day of our lives there occurs in us something of that evolution of our species which is still in full career. In fact every individual life, indeed every day in the life of an individual, *has* to represent a part, however small, of this evolution, a chisel-stroke, however insignificant, on the eternally unfinished statue of our species. For the whole of its tremendous evolution consists of myriads of such insignificant chisel-strokes. And so at every step we have to change, overcome, destroy the form which we have had hitherto. The resistance of our primitive desires, which we encounter at every step, seems to me to have its physical correlate in the resistance of the existing form to the shaping chisel. For we are at once both chisel and block, overcoming and overcome—there is a real, continuous *self-conquest*.

But these considerations will perhaps mean no more than a poetical playing with words, attractive to some and, because of their vagueness, repellent to others, unless we combine them with the views, developed in the previous chapter, of the association of consciousness with organic existence. At first sight it is by no means obvious that it is actually the evolution of species which is mirrored in consciousness; one might well think that evolution merely proceeds on the side, as it were; that, in its immense slowness, it is somewhat irrelevant to the brief span of an individual life, and in any case does not enter into consciousness with any particular vividness.

But it was just *this* that we established as probable: that consciousness belongs 'just' to those organic events

The moral law

which are not yet fully 'worked in', not yet fully, heritably, fixed; that consciousness in the human soma belongs exclusively to brain-events *because* the brain (or parts of it) is that human organ which is engaged in development, the spearhead of evolution, so to speak; and that consciousness belongs to brain-events precisely *in so far as* they can still be modified by changing environmental conditions, that it is precisely and only these modifications which enter into consciousness, while they are still in process of being learnt—so as to become, much later on, fully acquired and unconscious possessions of the species.

Consciousness is a phenomenon of the zone of evolution. This world dawns upon itself only where and in so far as it is developing, bringing forth new forms. Stationary points escape the light of consciousness, become fossilised, and are no longer perceived except indirectly through interaction with evolving points.

But it follows from what has been said that *consciousness* and *conflict with oneself* are inextricably bound up together. This conclusion, which sounds somewhat paradoxical to ordinary thought, may be easily verified by reference to the utterances of the wisest men of all nations and ages; that is to the unanimous opinion of those individuals whose lives—within that brief flash of time which we can survey—have represented the most powerful chisel-strokes upon the human form, and who therefore, if our idea is right, will have borne the lion's share of that conflict, that resistance of the inherited form to its transformation.

As a typical example, in which we can see particularly clearly that self-control means the conquest of

Seek for the Road

inherited ancestral characteristics, I will remind the reader of the passage in chapter VI which describes the reactions of a civilised man to an insult, and I suggest that it should be read again at this point. Notice particularly the condition of exceptionally intense consciousness—usually called excitement—which accompanies the process, and which quite obviously connects with the fact that an inner conflict is taking place. For the man who is so fortunate in his temperament as not to have this atavistic tension at his throat will get much less excited on such an occasion—but so will the man who follows the ancestral advice without more ado and simply knocks his opponent flat.

But this is a typical example in another respect: it shows how a particular virtue can in the course of evolution be transformed into a vice which needs to be eliminated. For primitive man, not yet living in a political community, constant readiness to do battle for himself and his wife and children, who depended entirely on *his* protection, really was a magnificent virtue, and was bound, by natural selection, to reach the very highest pitch. We still find this virtue praised in the Homeric poems, and the custom of duelling has preserved this atavistic value-judgement down to quite recent times. Nowadays we call the ancient virtue rage; it has become a vice, as the gods of our fathers have become goblins and demons.

Though we may see after all this that our whole conscious life *is* in fact an evolutionary struggle with our earlier self, with which we are in permanent conflict, yet we still lack a basis for saying that it *ought* to be so, a basis for the ethical *value*-judgement, for the ethical

The moral law

demand 'Thou shalt'. For of course we are not advocating the childish opinion that the thought of evolution towards a higher goal is in some way the conscious inner reason or motive for the demands of virtue. It *might* be that, temporarily, just as belief in personal gods has been used temporarily as such a motive. But the demands of virtue are, as Kant emphasised, a *fact*—and we have to understand this fact, and not this or that motive, known from experience to be variable within the widest limits, which may be used to shore up those demands.

The biological key to this seems to me to lie in the following observation. The particular example given above showed that a special characteristic which was originally helpful to the species may become damaging to it in the course of evolution; in just the same way, an *egotistical attitude* in general is a virtue, helpful to the species, in an animal living in solitude, but becomes damaging to the species if it lives in community with others. Hence those with a long phylogenetic history of city-building, like ants and bees, have long since abandoned all egotism. Man, who is obviously much younger in this respect, is only beginning to do so; *with us this transformation is even now in progress*. It is bound to take place, with all the necessity of a natural law, for an animal which advances to the building of cities without abandoning egotism will not survive; hence only those builders of cities who achieve this transformation will continue to exist. Of course it does *not* follow from this that we *shall* make this transformation, for we are not *bound* to continue as a species; an individual *can* and most often *will* remain totally indifferent to this. But, on the other hand, it is a *fact* that for every normally constituted human being nowadays, unselfishness is the unquestioned *theoretical* standard of value, the ideal criterion of action—however infinitely remote his own actions may be from that criterion. In this very remarkable fact, almost inconceivable in its contrast with the actual behaviour of men, I perceive an indication that we are at the beginning of a biological transformation from egotistic to altruistic attitudes.

To me, then, this seems to be the *biological* role of the ethical value-judgement: it is the first step towards the transformation of man into an *animal sociale*.

But let me say once more: I was not trying here to show forth the motives of ethical action, to exhibit a new 'foundation for morality'. Schopenhauer, we know, did that, and it is scarcely likely that in this direction there will be anything essential as yet to add to what he said.

WHAT IS REAL?

1960

I
REASONS FOR ABANDONING THE DUALISM OF THOUGHT AND EXISTENCE, OR MIND AND MATTER

Probably for historical reasons of language and education, it comes naturally to the simple man of today to think of a dualistic relationship between mind and matter as an extremely obvious idea. He finds no difficulty in thinking that we first, through our will, move parts of our living selves, and then, by means of them, move other material things; nor that material things, coming in contact with our bodies, give rise through the nerves to the feeling of touch; that vibrations in the air, when they reach the ear, cause the sensation of sound, and that light, striking the eye, causes that of sight, and so on (meaning that similar things apply to sensations of smell, taste and temperature). But a more careful consideration should make us less ready to admit this interaction of events in two different spheres—if they really are different spheres; for the first (the causal determination of matter by mind) would necessarily have to disrupt the autonomy of material events, while the second (causal influence on mind of bodies or their equivalent, for example, light) is absolutely unintelligible to us; in short, we simply cannot see how material events can be transformed into sensation or thought, however many text-

What is real?

books, in defiance of Du Bois Reymond, go on talking nonsense on the subject.

These shortcomings can hardly be avoided except by abandoning dualism. This has been proposed often enough, and it is odd that it has usually been done on a materialistic basis. Probably the first such attempt was the naïve suggestion of the great Democritus that the soul too consists of atoms, but of peculiarly subtle, smooth, spherical and hence highly mobile ones. (This was not wholly without repercussions, as appears from the famous fragment, Diels 125, discovered as late as 1900 amongst the writings of Galen.) Epicurus and Lucretius took this idea further, adding the delightful 'improvement' of 'atomic fits', usually attributed to the former, which were frankly supposed to explain free will in men and animals and have, in this connection, found a remarkable parallel in our own day. The monism of Haeckel and his school is another scarcely pardonable attempt, which casts a shadow over their services to science. Spinoza's uniting of the two in *one* substance which he called God, with the two attributes known to us of extension and thought, while avoiding the worst mistake, since it explicitly excludes interaction, nevertheless seems to us, greatly though we esteem that extraordinarily lovable and utterly honest and selfless thinker, a somewhat formal solution. Bertrand Russell, in *The Analysis of Mind*, made a promising contribution by suggesting that mental states are constituted from the same kind of elements as bodies, merely put together in a different way. The explanation offered here is most closely related to this. But it strikes me that Russell soon shies away from that fundamental

Abandoning dualism

surrender of the notion of the real external world which, alien as it seems to everyday thinking, is nevertheless absolutely essential. He soon lets the external world come back; probably so as to avoid having to see the wide sphere of overlapping in our different fields of personal experience, as the marvel which it really and permanently is.

But this is no good. If we decide to have only one sphere, it has got to be the psychic one, since that exists anyway (*cogitat—est*). And to suppose that there is an interaction between two spheres involves something of a magical, ghostly sort; or rather, the supposition itself makes them into one single thing.

After the important contribution quoted above (*The Analysis of Mind*, lecture v, 4th ed., 1933), according to which the physical and the psychical consist of similar elements, merely in different combination, the elements themselves being neither physical nor psychical, one is astonished to find the same great thinker, in 1948 (*Human Knowledge, its Scope and Limits*, part vi, chap. 6, p. 480), re-entering the ranks of those who inform us with quiet amusement that some thinkers actually *claim* to doubt the existence of the external world. Russell adds, almost with that kind of irony known as 'Irish bull', that in his opinion this position, while it cannot indeed be refuted, cannot really be adopted, even by those who assert it. (It strikes me that these two statements are so mutually contradictory that it is impossible to entertain even the *supposition* that they might both simultaneously be true.) Moreover, solipsism and Leibnizian monadology are not the *only* positions involved; they are the examples quoted, per-

What is real?

haps in order that these, the two weakest forms of monistic (or quasi-monistic) idealism, may serve to establish beyond question the master-debater's always irresistible powers of conviction.

It seems to me that the wish to reduce the whole of reality to mental experience has much deeper foundations than a mere obstinate desire to deny an idea (that of the real external world) without which we cannot achieve a single step in practical life. This *idea* is itself a mental construct and is not being questioned in the least. We are merely in the first instance setting ourselves against the assertion that there must also, externally to it or alongside it, exist an object of which it is the idea and by which it is caused. For this seems to me to be a completely superfluous duplication which offends against Occam's Razor. Further, we do not know what 'exist' is supposed to mean in this case—a concept which we do not need for the idea itself, since this is constructed, albeit in a very complex way, from the simple datum. And finally, any effective causal relation between that 'existent' something and the ideal world constructed of simple data would be an entirely new relation and very much in need of explanation, having nothing whatever to do with the nexus of causality within the ideal world; and this last, as we have known ever since Berkeley and even more clearly since Hume, is moreover less directly accessible to observation and altogether more problematical than Hume's philosophical successors, including even Kant himself, seem to have realised.

That was our *first* point. The second, no less important, is this. The idea which we are discussing—and

Abandoning dualism

which, as we have said, it would not occur to us to deny—includes my own body, despite that extra word 'external' which is customarily introduced when describing it. From this we see—just by the way—the inadvisability of locating a man's thoughts and ideas in his head, for one would then, amongst other things, be supposing that the whole external world was contained in a part of itself, which would certainly be appropriate, even if there were only one such head in existence. Now consider the following very general situation, which I will present, for the sake of vividness, as a concrete case. I am sitting on a bench in the park, absorbed in thought. Suddenly someone comes in front of me, seizes hold of my left leg above the knee and squeezes it fairly strongly, which, while not exactly painful, is unpleasant. I look up to see whether this is a joke on the part of some friend of mine and see, on the contrary, a dirty adolescent of repulsive appearance. I wonder for a moment whether a box on the ear will meet the case, but decide against it, collar the boy and march him along to a policeman who makes his appearance at that moment at the end of the path.

Now most of us hold the opinion that this whole process could be causally worked out within our idea of the external world and, if the idea were sufficiently complete, could be understood, that is, reduced to generally established laws, without any reference to the sensations and thoughts which I have throughout the whole little scene. We do *not* think that a body in the external world, that is, the urchin, evokes in my mind, through the conduction of the nerves, a feeling of being squeezed; that then the aforesaid mind, after receiving

What is real?

further information from the external world and briefly considering it, gives an order to its arm to seize that body in the external world by the scruff of its neck and propel it along to the policeman who has just been observed at the end of the path. You do not *have* to agree with this; you may regard the first mentioned, so to speak natural, explanation, lying wholly within our idea of the external world, as a prejudice; but even if you do not agree with it you must admit it as a heuristic hypothesis. Many people think it the simplest and hence—Occam's Razor again—the inevitable explanation, because nothing is known of any interaction between mind and body, in connection either with sensation or with voluntary movement. But then we have the danger of reducing the series of psychical experiences to a mere accompaniment of the physical events, which would take place just as well without it as with it, since they take care of themselves and do not need any psychic supervisor—in other words the danger of reducing everything that is important and interesting to us to a superfluous sideissue, which might just as well not be there, so that one does not really know what it is there for. I say that this danger arises if we forget that the causal nexus that we are talking about is situated in our *idea* of the external world—if we insist on locating it in a self-supportingly 'existent' external world not dependent on our psychic experience. It seems to me that this brings us to a somewhat paradoxical conclusion: if, without involving ourselves in obvious nonsense, we are going to be able to think in a natural way about what goes on in a living, feeling, thinking being (that is, to see it in the

Abandoning dualism

same way as we see what takes place in inanimate bodies)—without any directing demons, without offending against, say, the principle of increase of entropy, without entelechy or *vis viva* or any other such rubbish—then the condition for our doing so is that we think of *everything* that happens as taking place in our *experience* of the world, without ascribing to it any material substratum as the object *of which* it is an experience; a substratum which, as the rest of this investigation will show, would in fact be wholly and entirely superfluous.

II

LINGUISTIC INFORMATION AND OUR COMMON POSSESSION OF THE WORLD

I get to know the external world through my sense-perceptions. It is only through them that such knowledge flows into me; they are the very material out of which I construct it. The same applies to everyone else. The worlds thus produced are, if we allow for differences in perspective, etc., very much the same, so that in general we use the singular: world. But because each person's sense-world is strictly private and not directly accessible to anyone else, this agreement is strange; what is especially strange is how it is established. Many people prefer to ignore or gloss over the strangeness of it, explaining the agreement by the existence of a real world of bodies which are the causes

What is real?

of sense-impressions and produce roughly the same impression on everybody.

But this is not to give an explanation at all; it is simply to state the matter in different words. In fact, it means laying a completely useless burden on the understanding. The broad measure of agreement between two observed worlds, let us say B and B', is to be explained by some sort of correspondence with the real world, R, that is of B with R and of B' with R. Anyone who thinks like this is forgetting that R has not been observed. No one perceives two worlds, one observed and one 'real', no one is in a position to establish any sort of similarity in their structure. Or is R, while unobservable, a permissible hypothesis? I tried to show in the last chapter what a high price has, in my opinion, to be paid for this hypothesis. But in any case, even if admitted, it fails entirely to connect with anything. So you can say if you like that these two worlds of experience, yours and mine, agree because the same mould is shaping them similarly in similar material (which, by the way, is a very peculiar transfinite inductive conclusion, *sui generis*); but for the empiricist the heart of the question is: how do we both get our knowledge of this agreement? The empty hypothesis of reality does nothing whatever to help here. But the knowledge is there, really there, as real as the private worlds themselves. We want to know where it comes from. This is a valid question: how do we come to know of this general agreement between two private worlds, when they admittedly are private and always remain so? Direct comparison does not help, for there is none. It is absolutely necessary that we should start

Linguistic information

by being deeply troubled by the monstrous character of this state of affairs, if we are to treat with indulgence the inadequate attempts that have been made to explain it.

Some may feel tempted to retort sharply at this point, to the effect that this is all a lot of stupidity: isn't there in fact an extremely strict correspondence, even to the very details, between the content of any one sphere of consciousness and any other, so far as the external world is concerned? Well, well; and who is going to be the one to establish this correspondence?

What does establish it is *language*, including everything in the way of expression, gesture, taking hold of another person, pointing with one's finger and so forth, though none of this breaks through that inexorable, absolute division between spheres of consciousness. The pre-eminent significance of language, of a common language, is luminously clear (Ludwig Wittgenstein). I am now, perhaps, expected to go on to the platitudinous tale of how we arrive at the personalities of others as an analogical conclusion; but the tale is no more than a half-truth at best: when a baby, whose whole world is his mother's smile, gives her a friendly little slap, he is certainly not drawing any analogical conclusions. What is true, of course, is that only a minute fragment of what any one of us may call our picture of the world is drawn from our own sense-experience, the greater part coming from other people's experience plus communication (of which the lion's share is often not living communication but language as preserved in writing and print).

It is the hardest task, if not the only task, of a theory

What is real?

of knowledge to conceive, starting from scratch, how any kind of route can be constructed for mutual understanding, *without* in the slightest degree breaking through that privacy and separateness on which we have touched so often—for that is impossible. Once this were understood, it would be possible to construct some kind of picture of the genesis of a real language and its development to such a point of perfection as, say, Attic Greek; the details of the picture do not matter in the first instance. The predominant role in the first achievement of understanding may have been played by the introjection of will into other personalities; the very beginning of language consists surely not in imparting anything but in more or less violent expressions of desire—exclamations, pleas, commands, warnings, threats, and the like.

I want to examine more closely the reasons why I think it is incorrect to say that we arrive at, or even merely guess at, other personalities only by analogy, that is, by similarity of shape and behaviour. It is not only in his mother and other people around him that the child sees personalities, but also in animals, which are often bound to him in close mutual friendship, and even in things in his environment—he smacks the corner of the table when it hurts him. Similarity of shape or behaviour scarcely matters. He grieves for the flowers withering in a vase—and so indeed do we. It seems altogether preferable to see it precisely the other way round: it is natural to man to regard his whole environment as alive, as willing and consciously feeling; it is only gradually, as we learn from prehistory and history, that he sorts out the not-really-sensitive from

Linguistic information

the alive, and if, like Descartes, he considers himself exceptionally clever, he even goes a trifle too far. It is not only primitive man who thus attributes a soul to the thunderstorm and to his fetish; in the imagination of the cultivated Greek, nature is populated too, at least with fabulous beings:

> These heights were thronged with oreads,
> A dryad lived in every tree,
> And from the urns of lovely naiads
> Sprang the silver foam of streams.

Thunder and lightning, experienced always afresh in all their sublimity, were manifestations of the will of a wrathful Zeus. The oldest of the Greek philosophical schools, and in many respects the most matter-of-fact of them, the Ionians, were even in antiquity called the hylozoists, because they regarded all *matter* as *alive*; which of course need not necessarily have meant as much as 'having a soul'.

Now how do we, in all seriousness, make the distinction between (sensitive-) living and non-living? If we could give a reasonable answer to this, we should have the key to the question propounded above: how is it that, despite the separateness and privacy of our spheres of consciousness, which must be ruthlessly asserted, despite their being hermetically sealed against each other, there can nevertheless come to be an understanding between them, which can then attain to that perfection and subtlety which we encounter among cultivated human beings? At first sight this seems as impossible as the deciphering of Egyptian documents before the discovery of the Rosetta Stone.

It has been said: that is alive which moves of itself.

What is real?

This definition is not only useless to us but deceived Plato and Aristotle, for instance, into thinking that the heavenly bodies were gods; while Anaxagoras, who did not share this opinion, would have found that it cost him dear but for the timely action of his friend and pupil, Pericles, in getting him out of prison and away. As we know, the glorious free republic of Athens, in which all men were equal (until you got down to the slaves who actually did the work which kept the state in being)—this model republic was not, as we know, without its dangers for those who thought clearly and said what they thought (this description does not really apply to Plato, and Aristotle too died in exile in Euboea). But this is by the way.

It seems to me that the situation is as follows: a person first learns to know his own body as the only body in the external world whose movements, in a large number of cases, he controls at will, or, if preferred, the initiation of whose movements he knows in advance with some certainty, as soon as he wants them and approximately in the form in which he wants them. He then regards another body as sensitive and alive if, when he himself touches it with his own freely moved body (usually his hand), it does *not* normally perform predictable movements, that is, the kind which are familiar to him, from other occasions, as obviously communicated by the movement of his own hand when, for example, he pushes things away, sweeps them off the table, throws them into the air, and so on. We must add straight away that this 'testing for aliveness' is not only done by touching but in many other ways as well, of which the following are probably the most frequent:

Linguistic information

one moves one's hand, or something held in it, in front of the eyes of the object being investigated (if it seems to have eyes), or one shouts or whistles at it. And in each case the reaction indicating life may itself be a vocal sound or a change of colour or shape, and so on.

Simple and trivial though all this may be, it still seems to me important to realise that this can give rise to a linguistic understanding, in the widest sense, with the *alter ego*, despite the fundamental impossibility of transcending the limits of one's own consciousness. We will now go on to the sort of way in which that understanding may be achieved, considering, for simplicity's sake, the case which is most important to us: that in which the other body is of very similar construction to one's own; in other words, when the two individuals are of the same sort, and in particular when they are two human beings. What will then be observable is a repeated simultaneity of one or several movements (or noises, etc.) of one's own body with certain movements (or the equivalent) in the other, and perhaps with a third event. An important role is played here by the so-called imitative instinct, constantly observed in children, monkeys and even adult human beings, 'doing as the other one does'. At its most trivial, there is the yearly change in the fashion of clothes and warpaint; over longer periods, changes of fashion in speech condition the gradual alterations in a language. It is not necessary here to look for the reasons for this bias towards imitation; it will easily lead to the result that the two (groups of) movements, those of one's own body and those of the other one, become very similar to each other; for example, after attracting attention by means

What is real?

of touch, both will point their fingers at a third object (a dog) saying 'Bow-wow'.

First of all, a few annotations on this. Becoming aware of simultaneity is of fundamental importance, even in orientating one's own body in its position in its environment; through what is simultaneously seen, touched and perhaps heard, an idea of unified space is built up, in which the parts of our own body and of other objects in our environment are located. One can go into too many details, but I should perhaps offer an excuse for retaining the usual term 'environment', in spite of the fact that my reckoning of one's own body as part of it leaves it with nothing to environ (nor would 'surrounding world' be much better). Secondly, words like bow-wow and others in baby-talk, words in primitive languages like beri-beri, tom-tom, tsetse, etc., possibly even the reduplication of Indo-European verbs, and the pleasure taken in alliteration, assonance and rhyme all seem to me to bear witness to the inclination towards repetition of sounds, in these cases those made by oneself. Thirdly, the Berlitz method of teaching languages, which is said to be successful, more or less follows, I gather, the scheme roughly sketched above, and avoids basing itself on any existing common knowledge of any other language in the teacher and pupils. Fourthly, a child certainly learns its first language by the Berlitz method, usually from its mother and elder brothers and sisters.

It is scarcely possible for any historical study of language to trace the way in which a more and more finely nuanced linguistic understanding was gradually built up, over many generations, from this primitive

Linguistic information

tendency towards imitation; for the history of a language is, in the nature of things, bound to begin long after the fulfilment of what we should so much like to know about in its earliest stages and beginnings. The same applies to the history of human culture in general. But just as we have discovered among, for instance, the present inhabitants of New Guinea representatives of the Stone Age, though this lies far back in the past elsewhere, so the languages studied by ethnographers are also bound to be at very different levels of development. Personally, in considering the few languages of which I have any knowledge at all, even by hearsay, what strikes me most strongly is that venerable *ancient* languages such as Sanskrit, Greek, Arabic and Hebrew do not have the simplest grammar but the most difficult; while what is beyond doubt the most advanced of all languages, English, has so alarmingly few actual rules that, on the one hand, any uneducated foreigner can easily learn to understand it and speak some mangled version of it, while, on the other, only the greatest minds in the nation itself, men like Sir Charles Sherrington, Bertrand Russell or Gilbert Murray, are capable of expressing themselves in it clearly, intelligibly and in such fashion as to delight the reader or listener.

Still, comparison with the way a child learns his first language from his mother and family may well offer us our best opportunity for an insight into the genesis of language, in the same way that the development of an embryo from the fertilised ovum affords us a certain representation, though by no means an accurate one, of the phylogenetic evolution of the species. The adult who learns by the Berlitz method could be regarded as

What is real?

an experiment in this field, in the way that Darwin himself constantly made use of the breeding of dogs, pigeons, horses or tulips to illustrate or give support to his principle of natural selection. But of course a Berlitz student is nothing like a blank sheet of paper. He already knows that he is living in the same world as his fellow-students, his teacher, and indeed the rest of mankind; he has already learnt at least one language, and in many cases knows, or has at least some sense of, what it is all about; moreover, the language he is learning usually has the same grammatical structure as the one he knows, at least in essentials, even if they are, say, Hungarian and Arabic, or Arabic and Swedish. (Bertrand Russell once pointed out—rightly, it seems to me—the risk of philosophical prejudices arising out of the sentence structure common to all developed languages: articulation into subject, predicate, direct and indirect object, etc. We can attribute to this, not only the obstinately lingering doctrine of *substantia et accidens*, but also the separation of subject and object in the observation of nature, upon which the last few decades have bestowed a halo of mystery, or rather, have bestowed it upon their mysterious and supposedly newly discovered non-separation. To it also we can attribute the giving of a new lease of life to the *identitas indiscernibilium*, regarded as covering something which in fact lies at a much deeper level, namely Pauli's principle of exclusion, which, incidentally, should be regarded as an approximation to a more general proposition laid down by Dirac; and no doubt much more besides.)

No reasonable purpose would be served here by giving free rein to dilettante fantasies about the early

Linguistic information

development of language, that is, about how understanding gradually improved. I was very much impressed by an idea which I read recently and do not want to leave unmentioned, though unfortunately I cannot say who the author was or where I read it.[1] The idea was that the oldest roots in a language go back to unconscious attempts at imitating external events by movements of the tongue, jaw, etc., and at emitting sounds with these speech-organs in that position (or state of movement). This is a bold generalisation of the idea of onomatopoeia, which has long been an accepted notion in philology (words like sough, hiss, howl; Hebrew beelzebul = lord of the *flies*; Italian zanzara = midge). The generalisation consists in applying the idea of an attempted imitation not only to sounds but to other characteristics of an event, such as upward or downward movement, penetration, restriction, undoing a restriction, putting something cross-ways, acting suddenly or gently and slowly. It is easy to deceive oneself here. There are many cases in which words in current use, almost all of which have a long history of development behind them, seem to lend themselves to this idea. Pairs of words like *fest* and *lose*, *starr* and *weich* (fast and loose, stiff and soft) would sound less appropriate with the meanings reversed, as would the English pair (which is almost internationally intelligible) Stop and Go, where the vowel in the first word is pronounced short whereas that in the second (corresponding to the green light) is a fairly long-drawn-out diphthong.

However this may be, it seems to me in any case that

---

[1] Probably a reference to R. A. S. Paget, 'Origin of Language', *Science News*, **20** (1951), p. 77.

What is real?

the impulse to produce sounds oneself in imitation of those heard from others, and perhaps of other observed events as well, forms the basis of mutual understanding, of the development of a language, of awareness that we all live in the same world. We see ourselves in each other as in a mirror, but in a very extended sense; for while a real mirror reproduces movement it does not imitate sounds, nor does the image in it allow us to take hold of it, whereas our 'extended' mirror image usually feels warm like our own bodies. A hare leaps from the bushes and races away; the other man and I both raise our arms to point at this moving phenomenon and are perhaps by now accustomed to emit the same sound as we do so—say, 'Wu'. This makes me aware that the 'Wu' is there not only for me but for the other man as well; if it is a bear or a gorilla, we use other syllables to take note of it and draw attention to it. Memory, that once-and-all within our own personalities, plays a decisive role in all this; I take this for granted without closer analysis at this point. Nor do I want to seem to be asserting, by referring the origin of community-feeling to language, that starlings chattering in their tree at evening, wide-ranging migratory birds, bees, barnyard fowls, and so on, have not arrived at learning that they live in the same world. On the contrary. They are far more advanced in this respect than many a poor self-assertive egoist of our species. But then the time is long past when one could venture—and still hope to be taken seriously—to make so arrogant an assertion as that we human beings are the only creatures with a language.

We started off by doubting for a moment, faced with the inexorable separateness of spheres of consciousness,

Linguistic information

and their total and impenetrable exclusion of each other, whether we could ever arrive at affirming that a certain part of our various currents of experience (the part which is called 'external') is similar, indeed almost identical. As soon, on the other hand, as we have grasped the possibility of reaching understanding on this point, and are lucky enough to possess, in the languages which we have at our command, the means to such understanding, we at once become inclined to over-estimate the degree of precision in this understanding and to forget its inescapable limitations. Yesterday, on page one of a highly respected Modern High German grammar, in paragraph one, which deals with 'The concept and nature of language', I read the sentence: 'Words consist of articulate...sounds, by means of which the corresponding idea is indicated by the speaker and comprehended by the listener.' I could not help pencilling in the margin, 'not always'. I was not so much concerned with the rather narrow definition, which takes no account of words like because, though, despite, without, etc. On page two, paragraph two, which is supposed to deal with the origin of language, I wrote the same words in the margin when I read the laconic statement: 'Thus thought is the basis and prerequisite of language' (Karlsruhe: Friedrich Blatt, 1895). At the beginning of an essay[1] on a subject closely connected with our present one Boltzmann tells a story of how he asked in his school library

---

[1] *Wiener Berichte*, 106 (2a), (1897), 83. Also published in Ludwig Boltzmann's popular writings, no. 12 (Leipzig: J. A. Barth, 1905), 'Über die Frage der objektiven Existenz der Vorgänge in der unbelebten Natur' ('On the problem of the objective existence of events in inanimate nature').

What is real?

for a book on philosophy (he thinks by David Hume) and was very disappointed to find that it was available only in English, which he did not understand. His brother, who was with him at the time, had often had arguments with him about Ludwig's ideal of the necessity, and possibility, of defining all concepts, with complete precision, when they are first introduced; which his brother declared to be unattainable. It was an ideal, incidentally, of which the great physicist never lost sight (despite the defeat suffered on this occasion), and to which he came as near as it is possible to do. But Ludwig's disappointment on this occasion gave his brother the chance of a shrewdly and penetratingly mocking blow: 'If the book does what you expect of it, the language can't matter—for every word would have to be clearly defined before it was used.' Incidentally, either Boltzmann was mistaken about the author (Hume), or someone had been pulling his leg. For I have never encountered anyone, either in that group of quite profound thinkers to which this Scotsman belongs or, in general, among those writers of a former age whom one still finds readable, who reasons away—I had almost said: 'chatters' away—so easily and uninhibitedly *and for that very reason remains so plainly intelligible* as does David Hume; all in a childlike confidence that words do explain themselves, without painstaking and hard-to-remember definitions, even when they are being used in rather more subtle senses than those of everyday speech, so long as one simply puts them in the right context; in other words, that syntax matters more than vocabulary, or, to quote Goethe:

Linguistic information

> With little art, clear wit and sense
> Suggest their own delivery;
> And if thou'rt moved to speak in earnest,
> What need that after words thou yearnest?[1]

My friend Professor John Synge, who is a very amusing conversationalist as well as a mathematician, has written a little book for the general reader called *Science: Sense and Nonsense* (London: Jonathan Cape, 1951), in which, in the first chapter, called 'Vicious Circles', he uses what is called the *circulus vitiosus* to make mild fun of one-language dictionaries such as the *Concise Oxford Dictionary*, without of course wanting to deny their great usefulness to those who know the language concerned. You look up some word in a dictionary of this sort. It is explained by means of three or four or five other words in the same language. You look up each of these in the same dictionary. And so on. Since it only contains a finite number of words, a word must necessarily repeat itself sooner or later. In practice this happens after only very few stages. But this at once shows that the first explanation of the word was logically inadequate, that is, that every line of the whole valuable book is, in strict logic, defective. The use of another language or—*horribile dictu*—of a picture is, so to speak, forbidden by the rules of the game. Another humorist, writing in the dictionary of the Spanish Academy, was also no doubt wanting to show up the grave solemnity of this game by means of a joke when he explained *perro* (dog), in contrast to the other common household animal, cat, by reference to that habit in the full-grown male of the species which is

[1] Goethe, *Faust*, scene 1; translated by Bayard Taylor.

referred to in the Austrian vernacular as *Haxelheben*. The joke is of course presented with the requisite degree of solemn pedantry:...*patas posteriores, una de las cuales suele alzar el macho para orinar.*

III

THE IMPERFECTION OF UNDERSTANDING

While perhaps too broad and interspersed with too many amusing asides, the foregoing description of how we arrive at mutual understanding and at the insight that 'we all live in the same world' must, it seems to me, be accepted as factual even by those who regard it as an eccentric whim to wish to deny 'reality' to this world that we have in common. If you will grant me that description, I will not quarrel over 'reality', at least not until I have to. 'Reality', 'existence' and so forth are empty words. All that matters to me is this: suppose you do see it as necessary to refer the broadly shared character of one part of our experience (the part we call external) to the idea that the same die applied to similar 'malleable surfaces' will tend to produce similar structures, you still ought not to suppose that this can either explain or guarantee our awareness of this shared character. If you suppose that there is a real external world which is the active cause of sensation and which can consequently be influenced by our voluntary actions (an idea which I recommend you to avoid), then the

Imperfection of understanding

danger arises of going on from this plausible explanation of our common experience to regarding our knowledge of it as obvious, inevitable and complete, and to stop being concerned about its origin or the degree of completeness to which it can attain. To do so is simply wrong; this is no mere dispute over words.

It has often been said that knowledge of nature can never reach its goal; that one should never ask concerning any theory *whether* it needs to be modified, but merely in what direction; that, as Lessing said, the joy of intellectual work lies not in attainment but in struggling towards an ideal which always hovers ahead of us. But when this is said of the so-called exact sciences, the predominant idea is probably that we can never arrive at a complete reconstruction of nature in mental images. What we are acknowledging and asserting here is something more: it is impossible to have so much as a completely certain, unambiguous mutual understanding between human beings; it is a goal which we are forever approaching but which we can never reach. *On this ground alone exact science is never really possible.* A quite accurate, but perhaps somewhat too weak, analogy for what is meant here, is to be found in the severe limitations affecting the fidelity and goodness of a translation from prose or from simple, unrhymed verse. In the case of important texts, such as Shakespeare's plays or the Bible, generations have wrestled with the task, being seldom quite satisfied with what has already been achieved—though this, of course, is partly connected with the constant and relatively rapid alteration of the language into which the translation is made. (When I was a child, the

What is real?

English words *bath* and *bathe* corresponded, respectively, to the German noun and verb *Bad* and *baden*; nowadays *both* of them mean *both* these German words, but the first refers to a bath in a tub and the second to a bathe in a river or swimming-pool. German as spoken and written a thousand years ago—and I mean German, not Gothic—is no longer intelligible without the help of a dictionary or a Modern High German translation.) I said that the analogy was accurate but perhaps too weak. Why too weak? Because, as I said once before, most languages in which we are interested share a very similar structure. But I once got hold of two different German translations of the Tao-te-king. As I remember them, it was only possible here and there to recognise that they were both concerned with the same little Chinese work. ('Little' here is not a term of denigration. A joker was provoked to an affectation of astonishment by the brevity of this famous text. Lao-tse is said to have written it while waiting for a customs clearance.)

There is an almost insurmountable barrier to mutual understanding, even at the highest educational levels, in regard to certain particular qualities of sense-perception. It is not a supremely important point, and attention has frequently been drawn to it before, so we need not linger over it for long. The question is often put, for instance: 'Is it really certain that you see the green of this lawn exactly as I see it?' The question cannot be answered, and one may well ask whether it has any meaning. Dichromats (often described, inaccurately, as partially colour-blind or red-green defective) see the whole spectrum as a band of colours of precisely that degree of complexity which a normal

Imperfection of understanding

trichromat can produce for himself by mixing light (not paint!) of two complementary colours, A and B, on a matt white surface so as to obtain all the combinations from pure, full A through neutral grey to pure, full B. This can be objectively established. But *how* the dichromat sees the furthest red and the furthest violet visible to him on the spectrum, *in comparison with the colour-sensations of the normal trichromat*, cannot of course be established at all. The theoretical supposition—if one is not going to dismiss as cock-eyed the holding of any such thing when it cannot, in principle, be established—was that the dichromat saw a deep yellow at the long-wave (red) end, that its depth decreased as far as the neutral point (grey), and that from there on he saw a gradually deepening blue. A young person who had dichromatic vision in one eye but normal, trichromatic vision in the other (which can be objectively established) confirmed this supposition—but the confirmation rests entirely on our confidence in their having spoken the truth. (*Note*: I have twice used the expression 'objectively established': the findings thus established do, of course, rest on reports made by test-subjects about the similar appearance of certain mixtures of light, but in these cases one can so to speak cross-examine the people tested, which will in any case be done in order to achieve more accurate measurements; thus misreporting, whether intentional or careless, is discovered, and the description 'objective' is justified.)

Being very unmusical myself, I had better refrain from speaking of sounds and noises in this connection. But I think it is the same story. The fact that we agree in our diagnosis of sounds as a horse neighing, rain

What is real?

pattering, a tin being opened, or starlings twittering; the fact that we can tell a piano solo from a 'cello solo; the fact that musical people have similar affective experiences when listening to some particular symphony, and can to a certain extent understand each other on the subject; the fact that people with absolute pitch give the same name to the same sound—none of this differentiates sound-perception from colour-perception, certainly not with respect to the point at issue here. There are, it is known, two essential differences between hearing and vision: first, it is possible, especially for a skilled person, to make a very exact analysis of a single sound, according to the presence and intensity of its overtones (not necessarily harmonic); and there is no *sound-synthesis*, that is, the same sound cannot be produced by various mixtures of pure sounds. The same colour, on the other hand, can in general be reproduced, quite indistinguishably, by an extraordinary variety of mixtures of spectral light, and this *colour-synthesis* plays a very important part in research into colour-perception. At the long-wave end of the spectrum (red to green) even the pure colours of the spectrum can be produced by mixing those on each side of them (for example, yellow from red + green), without the eye's being aware of any difference. This is the first great difference between the two senses. Here is the other: as a compensation, so to speak, for its lack of complexity in the quality of sensation, our eye distinguishes very sharply between the various directions from which light strikes it. This is the source of our sharply contoured field of vision, which starts as two-dimensional and then extends itself, chiefly through

Imperfection of understanding

bi-optic vision in interplay with the sense of touch, so as to become genuinely three-dimensional visual space. In the case of sound, while 'directional hearing' is not altogether lacking, it is rudimentary in comparison with 'directional seeing', and seems to come about through the combined working of both ears.

Even though it does not concern us very closely here, I cannot resist referring to the very different manner of seeing in insects, into which Professor Karl von Frisch[1] has been researching during the last forty years in a series of brilliant and tireless experiments, chiefly on bees. It has long been realised that directional seeing in insects is quite different from ours, on account of the numerous 'facets' of their eyes. Bees are trichromats as we are, but *their* area of vision extends so far into ultra-violet that they could easily be supposed, in *our* area, to have dichromatic vision, as we in fact have in the long-wave area (red to green) where pure yellow plays the part of the 'neutral point'. Von Frisch has also established that for bees the polarisation of light, which varies in a regular but very complicated way in different parts of the sky and at different times of day, is a biologically important means of orientation; to us it is entirely unnoticeable, but bees, with their composite eyes, can perceive it. What was even more astonishing to me was that the eyes of bees and flies can receive more than two hundred separate impressions per second, as against a maximum of twenty in ours. 'No wonder a fly usually escapes our attempt at swatting it,'

---

[1] See, for example, K. von Frisch, 'How Insects Look at the World', *Studium Generale*, x (1957), 204; 'Insects—Lords of the Earth', *Naturwissenschaftliche Rundschau* (October 1959), p. 369.

What is real?

comments Frisch, 'considering that it can follow the movement of our approaching hand in slow motion.'

Now to speak of something else. Most people take it quite calmly if one asks them whether they connect the five simple vowel-sounds with any particular colours, senseless though it may seem to say so. But the associations differ. For me they are: a—pale mid-brown, e—white, i—intense, brilliant blue, o—black, u—chocolate-brown. I think the connection is permanent; it is also probably quite without significance. Any discussion about 'who is right' would be completely meaningless.

All that has been said in these last paragraphs about sense-perception can perhaps best be summed up by saying that we can, at best, reach understanding about the *structure* of the world grasped by the senses, but not about the quality of the units of which it consists. This leads to a whole series of observations which seem to me important.

In the first place, this limitation on mutual understanding is not particularly irksome. One would almost wish to say that it does not matter at all, so long as one can achieve a clear, unhampered agreement about the structures. For it is these which are of genuine interest, both purely biologically and to the theorist of knowledge. My second observation is that this is especially so because the limitation of our mutual understanding to structures applies, I think, far beyond the domain of the world as grasped by the senses, indeed, to everything which we want to communicate to each other, and especially to scientific and philosophical thought-forms of a higher and of the highest kind. One

Imperfection of understanding

example of this—but only an example—is furnished by the axiomatic procedure in mathematics. It consists in stating, without proof, a series of basic propositions (axioms) about certain basic elements (for example, natural number, point, straight line, plane...). Examples are: 'Every natural number has one and only one successor' and 'Two different points always define one and only one straight line'. From these axioms all the propositions of mathematics (or of some particular part of mathematics) are then logically deduced, and they remain valid quite independently of any visual meaning which may have attached to the basic elements, and quite regardless of whether, with respect to that meaning, the axioms seem plausible or not (they merely have to be free from contradiction, which is often by no means easy to prove).

A particularly clear and simple example of this occurs in projective plane geometry. The basic elements are the point and the straight line. One basic concept is that of coincidence of one element with another of the other kind (the point lying on the line, or, which comes to the same thing, the line going through the point). Two of the axioms are that two different elements of one kind always both coincide with one and only one of the other kind. Four further axioms do not concern us much here, except that they too are symmetrical with respect to the two kinds of element. They state that: if three elements of one kind coincide with *one* of the other kind there is, amongst those of the first kind to which the same condition applies, one which is uniquely definable as the harmonic conjugate of the first three (it does not matter what this means: it is simply that

What is real?

after the addition of this harmonic fourth, each of the four is equally a harmonic fourth to the other three); finally: four elements of the second kind which coincide with any one of such four harmonic elements, if they also all coincide with a fifth element of the first kind, are also harmonic. These sentences will be easier to grasp if one substitutes 'straight line' for 'element of the first kind' and 'point' for 'element of the second kind', or vice versa. Because of the perfect symmetry of all its axioms, one can *always* interchange the words 'point' and 'straight line' in any correctly deduced proposition of projective plane geometry and still have a correct proposition, that is, one which is logically deducible from the axioms, the so-called *dual proposition*. Diagrams of a pair of dual propositions are in general quite different from each other; the propositions themselves have often been discovered independently at different periods by different thinkers, before the fact of duality had been realised, for example, Pascal's line and Brianchon's point.

This geometrical example is my third observation on the theme that not only in what we grasp with our senses, but also in our mental constructions, what matters is not the individual units but the structure; and that some measure of secure understanding is possible in regard to the latter, but not to the former. Now for my fourth observation.

Even today we find lurking all over the place, especially in textbooks for the young—obviously because accuracy is not normally cultivated in them—the 'traditional' legend that in our sensibly perceived environment, which for this purpose is best regarded as

Imperfection of understanding

really existing, we can easily and conveniently distinguish between two kinds of qualities, primary and secondary. The first are supposed to be concerned with shape, mutual position and movement, the second with everything else. With reference to the first set we can have full confidence in our senses; as for the others, they are an optional extra which we add on our own account. We could express it pictorially by supposing that we are presented with outline drawings which we can then fill in as we please with water-colours, as in a child's painting-book.

The attack on this prejudice began with Leibniz, but it dies hard. One should not try to prove it false: that can scarcely work, any more than one could refute the idea that somewhere among the extra-galactic nebulae there is a select spot where man-like beings with wings, in long white robes, are engaged in making sweet music and enjoying paradise.[1] In both cases the burden of proof rests on the defenders of so bizarre an assertion. There is no reason why the perceptions of shape and movement which we form of our environment should be supposed to inhere any more strongly in a 'really existent' world of bodies than those of colour, sound, heat, etc. Both kinds are really there in our world of sensation. The limitation of mutual understanding to structure would apply equally in *all* cases.

But now, how are we to understand the more or less complete identity of structure which our environment seems to have for almost all men, and indeed to a great extent for animals too. For if, for example, fire suddenly

---

[1] Lucretius, and possibly Epicurus, had a similar idea about the gods of Olympus.

What is real?

breaks out on the road in front of a rider, or an unexpected gulf opens before him, the beast he is riding shrinks back in fear just as he does himself, and this is only one example of thousands which could be listed. If one prefers not to refer this complete agreement to a world of bodies as its common cause, is one then obliged to regard all those events as simply miraculous, when we constantly find them repeated with never-failing certainty (apart from dreams and hallucinations)?

No. Not altogether.

IV

THE DOCTRINE OF IDENTITY: LIGHT AND SHADOW

At this point I feel it necessary to declare in advance that the ideas considered in this section are not meant to have the same *logical* force as what has gone before, but that I regard their *ethical* importance as much greater. I will freely and frankly admit at the outset that, from now on, not only am I not going to refrain from metaphysics, nor even from mysticism, but that they play an essential part in all that follows. Of course, I know perfectly well that this admission alone is enough to call down upon me a violent attack from the rationalist quarter, that is, from the majority of my scientific colleagues, from whom the most I can hope is

The doctrine of identity

that they will say, with a gently mocking smile: 'Don't impose that on us, my dear fellow; you know, it makes us very much more inclined than ever to accept the extremely obvious explanation of a material world as the cause of our common experience; it's unartificial, it's accepted quite simply by everybody, and it *has absolutely nothing metaphysical or mystical about it.*'

Against this anticipated attack my defence consists in a no less amicable counter- or preventive attack, namely, that the assertion italicised above is mistaken. In the preceding sections I have been trying to establish, *first*, that the hypothesis of a material world as the cause of our wide area of common experience does nothing for our awareness of that shared character, that this awareness has to be achieved by thought just as much with this hypothesis as without it; *secondly*, I have stressed repeatedly, what neither can be nor needs to be proved, that this hypothetical causal connection between the material world and our experience, in regard both to sense-perception and to volitions, differs *toto genere* from that causal relation which continues in practice, perfectly rightly, to play so important a part in science, even now that we have realised, with George Berkeley (b. 1685) and still more clearly with David Hume (b. 1711), that it is not really observable, not, that is, as a *propter hoc* but only as a *post hoc*. The first of these considerations makes the hypothesis of the material world metaphysical, because there is nothing observable that corresponds to it; the second makes it mystical, because it requires the application of an empirically well-founded mutual relation between two objects (cause and effect) to pairs of objects of which only *one*

What is real?

(the sense-perception or volition) is ever really perceived or observed, while the *other* (the *material* cause or *material* achievement) is merely an imaginative construct.

I have therefore no hesitation in declaring quite bluntly that the acceptance of a really existing material world, as the explanation of the fact that we all find in the end that we are empirically in the same environment, is mystical and metaphysical. Nevertheless, anyone who wants to make it can do so; it is convenient, if somewhat naïve. He will be missing a great deal if he does. But he certainly does not have the right to pillory other positions as metaphysical and mystical on the supposition that his own is free from such 'weaknesses'.

The first alternative position to be taken up in modern times was probably Leibniz's doctrine of monads. As far as I can understand it, he tried to base that broadly shared character of our experience to which reference has so often been made on a pre-established harmony (that is, an essential similarity laid down right from the start) in the course of events taking place in *all* the monads, which do not, for the rest, have any influence on each other of any kind; 'monads have no windows', to use the expression which has become current. Various monads—human, animal, and the one and only divine one—differ only according to the degree of confusion or clarity with which the self-same series of events is enacted in them. I would not have referred to this suggestion (the naïveté of which, so far as offering an *explanation* of anything is concerned, almost surpasses that of materialism) if I had not come across a very remarkable observation made

The doctrine of identity

upon it by Friedrich Theodor Vischer.[1] He writes, in so many words: '...for there is but one monad, mind, which is in all things; monad has no plural. True, Leibniz stopped short of the splendid consequences of his idea, since, in sharp contradiction with the very concept of the monad as a conscious (spiritual) unity he postulated a plurality of monads side by side, like so many dead things, with no communication between them—but what does that matter to us?' The words occur in a criticism of an analysis of various works, including Goethe's *Faust*, by H. Düntzer (Cologne, 1836).

'There is but *one* monad.' Then what does the whole of monadology turn into?—the philosophy of the Vedanta (or perhaps the more recent but certainly independent one of Parmenides). Briefly stated, it is the view that all of us living beings belong together in as much as we are all in reality sides or aspects of one single being, which may perhaps in western terminology be called God while in the Upanishads its name is Brahman. A comparison used in Hinduism is of the many almost identical images which a many-faceted diamond makes of some *one* object such as the sun. We have already conceded that we are here dealing not with something logically deducible but with mystical metaphysics—just like the acceptance of a real object-world (usually called an external world, but it includes one's own body).

As presented in the Vedas, this idea is thickly overgrown with references to bizarre Brahmanic sacrificial rites and foolish superstitions, as anyone can see who has

[1] *Kritische Gänge*, II, 249, Verlag der Weissen Bücher (2nd ed., Leipzig, 1914).

What is real?

recourse to what are the best sources available in German, P. Deussen's *Sechzig Upanishads des Veda, aus dem Sanskrit übersetzt* (Leipzig: Brockhaus, 1921) and *Die Geheimlehre des Veda. Ausgewählte Texte* (5th ed., *ibid.* 1919). We do not wish to give any account of such things here. But setting them aside, it seems to me that the really serious conclusions drawn by the Indian thinkers from this 'doctrine of identity' are two, one ethical, to which we should be glad to subscribe, and one eschatological, which we must, I suppose, reject. The ethical conclusion is contained in the following metrical translation into German which occurs somewhere in Schopenhauer's writings, though I am not sure whether it comes from the Vedanta or the Bhagavadgita, which is inspired by the same spirit:

> Die eine höchste Gottheit
> In allen Wesen stehend
> Und lebend, wenn sie sterben,
> Wer diese sieht, ist sehend.
> Denn welcher allerorts den höchsten Gott gefunden,
> Der Mann wird durch sich selbst sich selber nicht
>   verwunden.

> The one all-highest Godhead
> Subsisting in each being
> And living when they perish—
> Who this has seen, is seeing.
> For he who has that highest God in all things found,
> That man will of himself upon himself inflict no wound.

Or in Latin:

> Qui videt ut cunctis animantibus insidet idem
>   Rex et dum pereunt, hand perit, ille videt.
> Nolet enim sese dum cernit in omnibus ipsum
>   Ipse nocere sibi. Qua via summa patet.

The doctrine of identity

(Both quoted from memory.) These beautiful words call for no commentary. Mercy and kindness towards all living beings (not only our fellow-men) are here praised as the highest attainable goal—in very much the same sense as Albert Schweitzer's 'reverence for life'. Schweitzer has often stressed that this supreme goal cannot in fact be attained without bringing about one's own death, and that of others, by starvation. He is, so far as I know, the first man ever to have included the plant world in this universal moral law, and not contented himself with a lukewarm vegetarianism as many do—who often go on to say that 'in our harsh climate one could not actually carry it out without damage to health'. It is even told of the great Gautama Buddha that he did not object to partaking of a meat meal with friends, if it was already prepared when he arrived, because the animal whose flesh he ate had not been killed simply on his account. An attitude of this kind can at least win our esteem for its honesty. I expect that many of us would do without meat if we could only have it, or offer it to our friends, on condition that we were prepared to take our turn at killing a calf, or a pig, or an ox, or a deer, fish or fowl. The fact that for the Hindu the callings of huntsman and fisherman rank in the next caste above the 'Untouchables' does not strike one as unintelligible, but only as hypocritical and discreditable, since the Hindu does *not* abstain from flesh-meat (the Buddhist does, but for him there is no such thing as caste). As for the condemnation that must fall, in this connection, upon those who hunt and fish for pleasure, often involving agonies of exhaustion and appalling terror for the little victims of their pursuit,

What is real?

we will not speak of it here; nor of the unspeakable cruelty of stuffing a goose for weeks on end in order that its liver may become pathologically enlarged and taste so very delicious; nor will we investigate more closely what right people have, when they live in countries where things of this sort are calmly accepted, not forbidden, but tacitly approved, to get heated over the 'medieval savagery' of bull-fighting, which certainly is cruel, not so much to the bulls (from all that I have heard) as to the poor old horses, but certainly is not more cruel than hunting or making *foie gras*, or, for the matter of that, the confining of worn-out horses for days on end in cramped stalls on board ship, so that they can be sent from countries that don't have bull-fights to others where, for some reason unknown to me, their transformation into potted meat produces a higher over-all profit. (As for what becomes of the corpses of the weakest animals, who die of being thrown about in the stalls in a rough sea with no one there to help them, this must remain a professional secret.)

So much for the ethical conclusion drawn by Indian philosophy from the (unprovable) thesis that we living beings are all simply sides or aspects of one single Being; a conclusion with which, as I have said, I, with Albert Schweitzer, am very willing to agree.

The other conclusion, the eschatological one, meets us at every turn, but it can be adequately gathered from this quatrain from the Brihadaranyaka Upanishad 4, 4, 19, translated by Paul Deussens as:

> Im Geiste sollen merken sie:
> Nicht ist hier Vielheit irgendwie;
> Von Tod zu Tode wird verstrickt
> Wer eine Vielheit hier erblickt.

The doctrine of identity

(In Mind, this is to be noted: there is no plurality here whatever; he who sees any plurality here is ensnared from death to death.)

Some explanation is needed here. Underlying it, in the first place, is the belief, deeply rooted in Brahmanism, in the transmigration of souls, which is in general much more widespread than might be thought by those born into an environment in which it is firmly rejected. Equally, in contrast to the whole tradition in which we have grown up, to the Brahmin the prospect of 'survival after death' is not a consolation, but rather a source of distress.[1] One's role and destiny in one's next birth are thought to be determined by the sum total of all one's deeds and omissions in all the preceding ones (*karma*). While this kind of 'justice' bears a certain resemblance to that believed in in other religions, it leads, in comparison with, say, Christianity, to a certain tranquillity, not to say indifference, in face of the inequality with which the goods of this life are apportioned. It is explicitly aristocratic, knowing nothing of the 'equality of all men before God'. If you are born a Brahmin (which does not by any means imply that you are very rich) this honourable rank (even if you are poor, and the servant of another Brahmin) is your due on account of your merits acquired in earlier births; if you are a Sudra (untouchable) or, for the matter of that, a hare or an ugly toad, you have brought it on yourself as a reward for the evil you committed in an earlier existence. It is a belief which allows the world to appear just despite

[1] A parallel to this can be found in the Rome of the first century B.C. Dread of frightful punishments in hell had taken such a hold on people that Lucretius Carus tried in his famous didactic poem to convey the comforting conviction that death really was the end of everything.

What is real?

its obvious injustice. It bears a certain resemblance to the feudal nobility, in which past generations take the place of previous births. You are an earl or a duke because one of your ancestors deserved well of king and country and was ennobled, and because his heirs, down as far as you, have at least not compromised themselves to the point of being deprived of their nobility by the king; indeed, it is probable that in the pre-eminent position which they occupied they have actually served their country in ways for which an ordinary citizen seldom has the opportunity.

Of course, the question of how a poor toad can work its way up, by moral conduct, to being a hare, and then become at least a Sudra, is a problem in itself.

All this is only a preliminary commentary, and not the content of the lines quoted above. As I said before, the endless cycle of birth and death and rebirth is for the believer in Brahmanism a source of distress. One's goal is to end it and to enter, by 'liberation', into a state which is compared in the Upanishads to a deep and dreamless sleep, called by Buddhists Nirvana and by Christians and many mystics an entry into or union with God. The comparison with a deep and dreamless sleep makes one ponder: how is this really different from the idea that 'death is the end of everything' of Lucretius Carus? In my opinion (I do not know whether it could be found explicitly stated in any of the ancient texts) what underlies this idea is the feeling of deep satisfaction, indeed of real bliss, with which a young man or woman who has been thoroughly tired awakens, full of vigour, after a long, deep, dreamless sleep. One feels and knows perfectly that one did not

The doctrine of identity

fall asleep only a moment ago, one is certain that many hours have gone by since then, but one can say nothing about them, one has no memory of them, except the certain feeling that they were good and indeed very good.

And now at last for the meaning of those four lines. 'There is no plurality here whatever.' This is simply the mystical-metaphysical doctrine of the Upanishads itself: the plurality of sensitive beings is mere appearance (*maya*); in reality they are all only aspects of the *one* being. The eschatology, which is really disturbing, is in the second half: the indispensable condition for liberation, that is, the ending of the eternal cycle of birth and death, is that one should genuinely appropriate this doctrine as one's own, understand it, and assent to it not only with one's lips but with one's whole soul.

This is disturbing indeed. It is 'salvation by knowledge'. It is even worse than, or at least quite as bad as, Luther's 'salvation by faith' (faith not being subject to the will) or Augustine's 'salvation by divine grace', in which, equally, the person concerned can do nothing about it one way or the other. Salvation by knowledge in the Vedanta is closely related to both of them. From the standpoint of one who himself accepts the doctrine of the Upanishads, salvation by knowledge is almost the worst of them, in as much as knowledge requires not only intelligence but also leisure for meditation. I say that this is almost worse than the sheer lottery of Augustinian election or Lutheran salvation by faith, which is much the same thing, since faith springs not from one's own merits but from divine grace. For

What is real?

knowledge, even of validly logical truth (and this is not what is called for here, but a mystical and metaphysical doctrine), is no mere lottery but a game with loaded dice; the advantage goes not only to the intelligent man but to the wealthy one, the man whose vital needs are attended to by others while he devotes himself to metaphysical speculation. On the other hand, of course, the Vedantic doctrine of salvation is to this extent much milder, in that its prospects are not limited to one single brief life. If it is not achieved in this one, the cycle goes on and on. And as to *how* it goes on, here one's own deeds and omissions (*karma*) are decisive. If one likes, one can suppose that 'good works' will thus obtain for one, in the end, a life in which intelligence, leisure and honest effort will lead one to grasp the doctrine of identity and so to attain salvation. Yet there still remains about it a certain flavour of 'the sole bestower of all blessedness'. But perhaps this is something that hangs about all real religions, good and bad alike.

Anyone who wishes today to adopt the Vedantic view of the world will above all be well advised to leave out the theme of the transmigration of souls. Not because Christianity denies it. For in the first place Christianity is much less widespread today than baptismal registers would lead us to suppose, and secondly we are the heirs of Hellenism at least as much as of the Sermon on the Mount, the earliest recorded text of which, for the matter of that, is Greek, not the classical Greek of Aristotle or Plutarch but that lovely, simple, popular tongue which for centuries after Alexander's conquests seems to have been the *lingua franca* of the eastern

The doctrine of identity

Mediterranean and the Near East. The idea of the transmigration of souls was by no means alien to the early Greeks, as we know from the Pythagorean tradition. But it is logically meaningless, if combined with that of a complete obliteration of memory. And in fact that school of thought did attribute to an exceptional person such as Pythagoras the fantastic power of remembering his earlier births; he is even supposed to have proved it by recognising things and places which he had never seen! It seems to me that it was felt that the claim to a *special* identity would collapse altogether without at least the possibility of remembering, if only occasionally and in exceptional cases. One thinks of so many things in this connection: the beautiful conception, which Plato's Socrates develops, of learning as a reawakening of what was once known but has been forgotten; and the important part played by *race*-memory in modern evolutionary theory and animal psychology. (And here I cannot refrain from recalling Richard Semon's two books: *Die Mneme* (Leipzig, 1904) and *Die mnemischen Empfindungen* (Lcipzig, 1909). On the biological side it was objected against Semon that there was little point in his drawing analogies between various other phenomena and memory, since memory itself is the least understood of all biological phenomena. To me this seems like saying that there is little point in affirming that atomic nuclei *all* consist of that 'amphibium', the proton-neutron, since these particles are things about which we know very little as yet.)

But in any case it seems bizarre that a human being who is living now and undergoing great distress, or for that matter a toad which is living now, should be atoning for the misdeeds of an evil-doer, now dead, of whom he or it has no recollection whatever. We cannot but eliminate this doctrine of *special* identity, and with it go both the aristocratic attitude and the idea of salvation by enlightenment from the cycle of births, because there is no such cycle. Nor, of course, can we save the pretended justice in the world-process. But we still have the lovely thought of unity, of belonging unqualifiedly together, of which, as quoted above in German and Latin, Schopenhauer said that it was his comfort in life and would be his comfort in death. And at the same time this idea, while itself no less mystical and metaphysical, fulfils the function of an external world considered as really existing; such an external world is still interesting—no more so than the world of our mind—but does not naturally lead to any ethical consequences.

V

TWO GROUNDS FOR ASTONISHMENT: PSEUDO-ETHICS

First let us summarise. We have found *two* remarkable states of affairs, each of which is in its way astonishing. It is important to make a very sharp distinction between these two findings, for, since very similar words are used to describe them, it is easy to confuse one with another. If the present study can be said to contain anything new, it will have been, chiefly, to have pointed out the necessity of separating these two findings.

Two grounds for astonishment

First, it is astonishing that, despite the absolute hermetic separation of my sphere of consciousness from all others (which no clear-thinking person denies) the origin and development of a common language, set in motion by the imitative instinct, as briefly sketched above, leads inevitably to the recognition of a far-reaching structural similarity between certain parts of our experiences, the parts which we call external; it can be expressed in the brief statement that we all live in the same world. This is a process whose course we can follow again and again in any growing child; it is not possible to have doubts about it, our danger is rather that custom will blunt our astonishment.

But there is something else, distinct from the marvellous way in which, despite the absolute separation of our spheres of consciousness, we become aware of our shared world—'we' being not profound and learned thinkers but children far below school age. This something else is the fact that, despite the separation of our spheres of perception, this extensive agreement or parallelism in what is called the external part of them *is there at all*. How? Or do we ourselves supply the parallelism, in the way indicated in the last section? Are you dreaming me and everything else, and am I dreaming you and everything else, so cleverly that our dreams match? But this is mere foolish playing with words.

We are dealing, then, with two amazing states of affairs. It seems to me that the first one is rationally and scientifically intelligible by reference to the ontogenetic and, where possible, phylogenetic origins of linguistic understanding. If it be said that this at once involves presupposing the second state of affairs, I will offer no

What is real?

contradiction. To me, what is essential is that this second matter is *not* rationally comprehensible. In order to grasp it we are reduced to two irrational, mystical hypotheses: either (1) the so-called hypothesis of the real external world, or (2) the admission that we are all really only various aspects of the One. I have no quarrel with anyone to whom it seems that these two really come to the same thing in the end. That is pantheism, and the One is called God-Nature. But this involves recognising, once and for all, the metaphysical character of the hypothesis in its first form (a real external world); this takes us miles away from vulgar materialism. The real ethical consequence can be more easily drawn from the second conception, the doctrine of identity.

It must be admitted that the doctrine of identity *looks* even more mystical and metaphysical. It makes the various degrees of sharedness in our experience less easy to understand. Suppose I live at no. 6 Park Street. A good friend of mine, who shares many of my interests, lives next door at no. 8. We meet each other three or four times a week, go out together, travel together, etc. (This and what follows is, alas, only imaginary.) We two are then living indeed very much 'in the same world'. This applies in a lesser degree to myself and another good friend, also interested in the same sort of things, who lives in Los Angeles; and also to myself and the excellent caretaker at no. 6 Park Street, who is a retired bank-clerk chiefly interested in stamps and football pools. But even if I have a dog, which goes regularly for walks with me, rejoicing over each one of them with the same idiotic barkings and leapings, there

Two grounds for astonishment

is a considerable bond between us, even an emotional one, since I would much rather take my constitutional with him than alone. But we come at last to cases like: I and David Hume; I and Friedrich Schiller; I and Democritus of Abdera; I and Xenophanes. The hypothesis of the real world does at least explain some of these very various degrees of sharedness in a natural way, because it includes the reality of space and time or, if you prefer, of space-time. The doctrine of identity requires some very penetrating thinking in order to make these distinctions plausible, thinking which has never yet, perhaps, been properly done. But this seems to me to be a minor defect beside the incomparably higher ethical content and the deep religious consolation afforded us in our ephemeral life by the doctrine of identity. Materialism offers neither; though there are many people who convince themselves that the idea which astronomy gives us of myriads of suns with, perhaps, inhabitable planets, and of a multitude of galaxies, each with myriads of such suns, and ultimately of a probably finite universe, affords us a sort of ethical and religiously consoling vision, mediated to our senses by the indescribable panorama of the starry heavens on a clear night. To me personally all that is maya, albeit maya in a very interesting form, exhibiting laws of great regularity. It has little to do with my eternal inheritance (to express myself in a thoroughly medieval fashion). But that is a matter of taste.

It must also be admitted that the mere sharedness of the world in which we live, no matter how it is understood in metaphysical terms, leads to a kind of ethics, which I will take the liberty of calling pseudo-ethics.

What is real?

Experience shows that, because of our sharing of one world, we can hurt each other a great deal physically, and psychically as well, and also, on the other hand, that we can help each other and make each other happy, if only by listening to each other. For we find that once linguistic understanding is established, people are very fond of talking, and sometimes even like to get answers. (The worst of all punishments is prolonged solitary confinement without books, which at least enable one to listen to the author, or writing materials, which at least make possible some potential communication with future readers.) In general, everyone stands to receive more happiness if those around him are kind to him than it will cost him if he in his turn is kind to others; conversely, he will get less pleasure out of hurting someone else than is worth the risk of having the same done to him by some third party stronger than he; and, furthermore, a certain natural mutuality can be counted on in all this. Therefore we can say that, exceptions apart, the effect of purely rational considerations is to produce mutually decent behaviour of human beings towards each other, and the appearance of a general inclination towards an ethical attitude. This pseudo-ethic is expressed in a number of popular proverbs, such as 'Do as you would be done by' or 'Honesty is the best policy'. Even 'Mit dem Hute in der Hand kommt man durch das ganze Land' (Hat in hand you can travel the whole world over) is not much better, for this comes near to requiring a hypocritical pretence of deference towards everybody and especially, no doubt, towards influential people. If you turn to what is perhaps the most famous novel in the whole of world

Two grounds for astonishment

literature and run through the utterances of Sancho Panza, which often consist of an almost unbroken tissue of folk-sayings, you will undoubtedly find plenty more such mottoes of pseudo-ethics, adding up to something that one might almost call utility morality. Of course, properly to appreciate the lovably comical quality in the long speeches of that good honest squire it is nothing like enough merely to have mastered the language; you would need to be familiar with the whole treasure of Spanish proverbial lore of that period (three or four centuries ago), which must have been very rich, and I expect still is so. A closer examination of this same splendid Sancho (which is out of the question here) might lead one to realise that it is possible for a man to be stuffed to the brim with utilitarian proverbs of this sort, and personally timid into the bargain, very fearful even of such decidedly unpleasant, but not really cruel, procedures as being tossed in a blanket, and still be a stout fellow ready to be beaten up and spitted for his master (if not without a good deal of moaning and groaning) if it absolutely cannot be avoided. So we had better not be too contemptuous even of pseudo-morality, such as arises from the usual hypothesis of the real world, with other selves like my own and so forth. It is better than nothing. But there seems to us to be more nobility in that other view, spoken of in the German and Latin verses on p. 96, which that poor pessimist Arthur Schopenhauer described as his comfort in life and in death. It is quite irrelevant whether Schopenhauer himself lived in accordance with this higher ethic. His notorious diary-entry, *'obiit anus, abiit onus'* tells against his having done so (it is said to refer to a charwoman whom he threw downstairs in a rage and to whom he was then obliged to make regular monthly payments). I would prefer personal contact with Sancho Panza rather than with Schopenhauer; he was the more decent of the two. But Schopenhauer's books are still beautiful—except when some superstitious madness suddenly breaks out in them. But this, as we learn from the later development of the ancient, beautiful, simple doctrine of identity in India itself, seems to be its sad fate: it is all too ready to open to any silly nonsense that comes knocking gently at the door. Indeed, 'miracle is faith's dearest child'. And the more fine, subtle, abstract and sublime that faith may be, so much the more fearfully does man's weak, fainting spirit snatch at miracles, however foolish, to be its stay and support.